Praise for
The Tao Made Easy

"There could be no better pairing of timeless truths and modern sage than that of Lao Tse and Alan Cohen. With the warmth and wisdom befitting these masters, Alan Cohen's *The Tao Made Easy* liberates both the ancient teachings of Lao Tse and the mind and spirit of his readers."

— Mike Dooley, *New York Times* best-selling author of *Infinite Possibilities* and *Playing the Matrix*

"In native cultures wisdom is transmitted through stories. The stories told around the evening fire can heal, inspire, and motivate. They are the power that holds a tribe together. Alan Cohen, in his splendid book *The Tao Made Easy*, allows us to access the wisdom of the Tao through his stories. Each story gleams like a jewel on the far horizon. Highly recommended!"

— Denise Linn, best-selling author of *Energy Strands*

"In Alan Cohen's accessible new take on the ineffable *Tao Te Ching*, the 'Tao that cannot be told' is now told with fresh insights and practical ways of being, according to the universal principles shared by all. This ancient wisdom has been brought to life for a new era deeply in need of enlightenment. Fresh insights, practical, easy entry, and immense delight!"

— Chungliang Al Huang, president-director, Living Tao Foundation and International Lan Ting Institute, and co-author with Alan Watts of *Tao: The Watercourse Way*

"As a lifelong Taoist practitioner, I was thrilled to read Alan's book *The Tao Made Easy*. It is filled with profound and perennial wisdom from *Tao Te Ching*, brought up to date for 21st-century spiritual seekers. Reading Alan Cohen's warm, funny, accessible, and infinitely wise take on an ancient spiritual masterpiece made my heart sing and my soul rejoice!"

— Jason Chan, Taoist Master, lifelong *A Course in Miracles* teacher, creator of *Infinite Arts*, and award-winning author

"In a magnificent fusion of ancient wisdom and real-world practical application, Alan Cohen has masterfully rebirthed the essence of the *Tao Te Ching* . . . inviting the Chinese sage, Lao Tse, into the heart of the readers and—in the process—awakening timeless healing energy to help us solve life's most pressing challenges. *The Tao Made Easy* truly touches the Soul!"

— davidji, author of *Sacred Powers*

THE
TAO

Made Easy

ALSO BY ALAN COHEN

CDS/DVDS/ONLINE COURSES

*Available from Hay House
Please visit:

Hay House USA: www.hayhouse.com®
Hay House Australia: www.hayhouse.com.au
Hay House UK: www.hayhouse.co.uk
Hay House India: www.hayhouse.co.in

***

THE TAO

Made Easy

Timeless Wisdom to Navigate
a Changing World

ALAN COHEN

HAY HOUSE, INC.

Carlsbad, California • New York City

London • Sydney • New Delhi

Published in the United States by: Hay House, Inc.: www.hayhouse.com* • *Published in Australia by:* Hay House Australia Pty. Ltd.: www.hayhouse.com.au • *Published in the United Kingdom by:* Hay House UK, Ltd.: www.hayhouse.co.uk • *Published in India by:* Hay House Publishers India: www.hayhouse.co.in

Cover design: Neil Swaab • *Interior design:* Nick C. Welch

The author of this book does not dispense medical advice or prescribe the use of any technique as a form of treatment for physical, emotional, or medical problems without the advice of a physician, either directly or indirectly. The intent of the author is only to offer information of a general nature to help you in your quest for emotional, physical, and spiritual well-being. In the event you use any of the information in this book for yourself, the author and the publisher assume no responsibility for your actions.

Library of Congress Cataloging-in-Publication Data

Names: Cohen, Alan, 1950- author.
Title: The Tao made easy : timeless wisdom to navigate a changing world / Alan Cohen.
Description: 1st edition. | Carlsbad : Hay House, Inc., 2018. | Includes bibliographical references.
Identifiers: LCCN 2017046125 | ISBN 9781401953621 (tradepaper : alk. paper)
Subjects: LCSH: Taoism.
Classification: LCC BL1920 .C556 2018 | DDC 299.5/1444--dc23 LC record available at https://lccn.loc.gov/2017046125

Tradepaper ISBN: 978-1-4019-5362-1
E-book ISBN: 978-1-4019-5363-8
Audiobook ISBN: 978-1-4019-5388-1

1st edition, July 2018

Printed in the United States of America

To Lao Tse,

for the blessed simplicity
he has breathed into the soul of the world.

CONTENTS

INTRODUCTION

An ancient Chinese blessing—or some say curse—wishes, "May you live during interesting times." That wish, for good or ill, has come true for us. Changes fire at us from every angle, and the future we planned for is no more. A survey revealed that more people believe that extraterrestrials are visiting Earth than believe their Social Security benefits will be there when they retire. The digital revolution has upended the book, music, and movie industries as we knew them, and required millions of workers to learn new skill sets or reinvent themselves. Online shopping is shutting down long-established department store chains, turning malls into ghost towns. That sweet couple next door is getting divorced, and we wonder if our own relationship may be next. Crazy people with guns open up fire in schools and churches. The news gets weirder daily, the world seems to be spinning out of control, and we reel at choice overwhelm. The faster we run, the harder it is to catch up.

Now what? How do we reconcile living in the best of times and the worst of times? Where do we find a compass to navigate a world for which we have no map? Is there some voice of wisdom that can override raging absurdity, assuage our gnawing insecurity, and give us a shred of hope?

There is. Even while upheaval and insanity appear to prevail, there exists rock-solid sensibility not subject to the winds of change, no matter how harshly they assault us. If truth were shakable by human frailty, truth it would not be. The answer to overwhelming complexity is not greater complexity. It is refreshing simplicity. The way we get out of this mess has to be different than the way we got in.

Twenty-five hundred years ago, a Chinese man called Lao Tse, which means "old master," was appointed by the king of the Zhou dynasty to the coveted position of keeper of the imperial archives. As time went on, Lao Tse grew frustrated and disillusioned with the war, divisive politics, and moral decay he observed, and he hungered for simplicity, harmony, and integrity. At an advanced age, he packed up and left the city to claim a saner, more natural life. As Lao Tse was about to pass through the western gate of the kingdom, a guard recognized him and beseeched him to record his wisdom before he disappeared. It was then that Lao Tse set brush to parchment and penned the 81 stanzas of *Tao Te Ching*, or "The Book of the Way of Virtue."

But the elder sage was writing not just for the people of his time. He was writing for us today. Behind our wireless connectivity, slick gadgets, and rocketing roadsters to orbit Mars, the same issues that plagued Lao Tse's world face us today: conflict between nations and religions, disease, starvation, greed, corruption, relationship angst, family breakdown, social unrest, and ethical decline. The old master's short book of only 5,000 written characters identifies the source of human suffering and its remedy, and stands as the most translated, interpreted, and printed book in history, with the exception of the Bible. With stunning brevity, Lao Tse implanted a time capsule of healing never more needed than now.

Yet while most readers recognize the profound wisdom imbued in *Tao Te Ching*, the language remains mysterious to many. Utter simplicity can seem confusing to the complicated mind. Add the difficulty of accurately translating ancient Chinese into modern language, and you can understand why many readers scratch their heads and wonder, *What does this have to do with me and my life?*

The answer is: *everything. Tao Te Ching* offers some of the most helpful insights in how to live ever recorded by a human being. His guidance can offset the ills of the modern world as well as the ancient. But to make the teachings work for us, we need down-to-earth application of broad-stroke truth, a contemporary voice to make the principles work in our daily experience.

That is something I can offer. I enjoy shining lofty ideas on nitty-gritty situations to elevate and heal them. After treading the spiritual path for many decades, I am tired of philosophies. All I care about is real-life examples that work.

I hesitated to dive into this undertaking because so many writers have penned translations and interpretations of *Tao Te Ching*. I did an Amazon.com search for *Tao Te Ching* and found 1,216 related books currently in print, including the revered translation by Gia-Fu Feng and Jane English; Dr. Wayne Dyer's popular *Change Your Thoughts—Change Your Life*; and the immortal surfer version, *Dude De Ching*. What could I possibly add?

I decided to take a different approach than any of the other Dudes De Ching I have read. Rather than marching through the stanzas and commenting on them verse by verse in a linear fashion, I have extracted the most significant themes of *Tao Te Ching* and applied them to life as we know it in the 21st century. How to deal with painful, confusing, or changing relationships. How to master money instead of letting it master you. How to keep your head on straight while fulfilling a demanding work schedule, then get the kids to do their homework, and then find some sleep instead of worrying about how you are going to pay your bills. How to deal with overbearing bosses or people who return kindness with cruelty. How to find solace in the face of the loss of a loved one. How to thrive in a healthy body. How to relate to politics that resemble an insane asylum run by delusional inmates. How to deal with dilemmas that seem new and different but are simply variations on themes that have plagued humanity since we all started trying to live together.

For these answers I call forth Lao Tse's disarmingly simple teachings on humility, integrity, ease, flow, and kindness as redeemers of a culture grown blind to virtue. Then I highlight key verses of *Tao Te Ching* to illuminate the principles of each chapter. Thus the classic text becomes a platform from which to live rather than a goal unto itself—precisely what the old master intended.

Soon after I began writing, I came to a verse I did not understand. *How would Lao Tse explain this?* I wondered. "Why don't you ask him?" a voice in my mind suggested. I was being guided to go directly to the master and take him as my mentor. If everything the sage wrote is accurate, his wisdom spans far beyond the bookends of time that encapsulated his body. The spirit of Lao Tse is alive and available to anyone who wishes to receive the benefit of his insight. Whether Lao Tse spoke to me personally or I simply tapped into the mindstream that guided him does not really matter. We are after truth, not personality.

As I continued to relate to Lao Tse as my personal tutor, an even more striking vision emerged: *What if I were his student, at his side when he walked the earth in ancient China, meeting with him daily, asking him penetrating questions, and learning from his example?* I visualized the old master standing in his kitchen serving me tea; correcting me when I painted myself as a victim; and comforting me when I had worked too hard. I could see him quietly tending herbs in his garden; counseling a young woman unhappy with her parents' choice for her husband; taking home a starving dog; confronting an arrogant politician; and hiking along a country road, a long slim stick of bamboo resting on his shoulder, toting a small cloth pack containing his few earthly possessions. Such scenes grew more vivid until I felt transported to the presence of the master. I had set into motion a kind of spiritual time machine that carried me back 25 centuries to sit at the feet of genius and bask in timeless truth.

Buoyed by my personal relationship with the elder sage, I infused these intimate vignettes into my writing. In each chapter you will find a dramatized scene that brings Lao Tse's teachings to life so you can practically reach out and touch him. Philosophy registers in our intellect; stories and images touch our inmost self. My goal in this book is to reach both your head and your heart. Thus you will experience *Tao Te Ching* from the inside out, and know the Tao as the master himself did.

Lao Tse doesn't just want us to read his book; he wants us to live his insights and use the changes coming at us to further our spiritual advancement. We may feel lost, but we are not forsaken. While part of us is mired in confusion and illusion, another part remembers what is real and will not rest until we reclaim our birthright and fulfill our destiny. Together we will find our way home. We will take the wisdom of the ages and make it our own. The domain we will enter is not one of time and space, but eternal truth. Behold the healing power of the Tao, which calls to you to receive its gifts in your life here and now.

A FEW NOTES TO THE READER

The Translation

All of the verses quoted in this book from *Tao Te Ching* are verbatim from the translation by Gia-Fu Feng and Jane English (2011 edition). I discovered the original version of this translation when I was in college, and the attractive volume has held an esteemed place in my home for the many years since that time. The grace of the text and the inspiring photos make this a classic that honors the Tao and Lao Tse. My deep thanks to the authors and the publisher, Random House, for their generous permission to quote this elegant text.

The Excerpts

This book contains many of the stanzas from *Tao Te Ching*, but not all of them. Stanzas were chosen that underscore the themes this book highlights. Each verse from *Tao Te Ching* appears once, with the exception of a few verses that bore import for different chapters.

The numbers at the conclusion of each excerpt from *Tao Te Ching* refer to the stanza from which the excerpt is drawn.

The Dramatized Vignettes

Each chapter contains a fictional depiction of interactions with Lao Tse at the time he lived and taught. These vignettes are not presented as factual, but as imaginative explorations of what a student of the master might have experienced in his presence. I have made an effort to include some details of daily life during the period of the Zhou dynasty around the year 500 B.C. If you find any historical inaccuracies or anachronisms, I ask your indulgence. These scenarios are not presented as actual events, but rather as a venue to showcase the themes and teachings of *Tao Te Ching* as taught and lived by the master Lao Tse.

WHAT'S
WITH YOU?

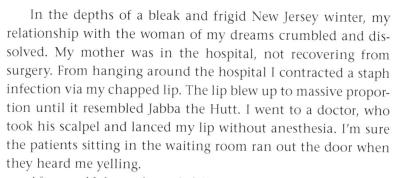

In the depths of a bleak and frigid New Jersey winter, my relationship with the woman of my dreams crumbled and dissolved. My mother was in the hospital, not recovering from surgery. From hanging around the hospital I contracted a staph infection via my chapped lip. The lip blew up to massive proportion until it resembled Jabba the Hutt. I went to a doctor, who took his scalpel and lanced my lip without anesthesia. I'm sure the patients sitting in the waiting room ran out the door when they heard me yelling.

Afterward I drove through falling snow to a pharmacy to get medication. When the people in line took one look at me, they all stepped aside so I could get to the counter immediately. Then I realized I had forgotten my wallet, and the pharmacist told me to just take the meds and go take care of myself. It was the toughest day of my life.

Until I arrived home. When I opened my mailbox, I found a letter from my beloved mentor, Hilda Charlton, the person I most respected. *"Dear Alan, I just want you to know how much I love you and I believe in you. You are doing wonderful things. Don't be put off by adversity. You are on the road your soul came to master. You have help from unseen sources. You are blessed and deeply loved. Hilda."*

During the 14 years I studied closely with Hilda, that was the only letter she ever wrote me. If I could scan all the days of my life and choose a moment to receive that letter, there is no question it would have been that day. Hilda had no idea what I was going through. She just acted on her intuition with impeccable timing. Compassion found me when and where I most needed it.

While it appears that the universe is a foolish, even cruel play of random events, there is an intelligence operating behind the scenes, a fabric of life that integrates all creation. This power is invisible to the eye, yet more real than anything the senses can touch. It is a mystery to the intellect but knowable to the heart. It is life itself. Lao Tse called this power "the Tao," or "the Great Way."

> *Something mysteriously formed,*
> *Born before heaven and earth.*
> *In the silence and the void,*
> *Standing alone and unchanging,*
> *Ever present and in motion.*
> *Perhaps it is the mother of ten thousand things.*
> *I do not know its name.*
> *Call it Tao.*
> *For lack of a better word, I call it great.*
> *Being great, it flows.*
> *It flows far away.*
> *Having gone far, it returns.*
> *Therefore, "Tao is great;*
> *Heaven is great;*
> *Earth is great;*
> *The human being is also great."*
> *— 25*

Already with You

We all know the benediction "May the Force be with you." Yet for all the kind intention this wish bestows, it is slightly flawed. It assumes that you must either get lucky or do something to get the Force to be with you. But the Force is *already* with you. It breathes, speaks, and acts *in* you, offers you guidance and grace at every turn, and expresses *as* you. Because you are a creation of the Force, it could no more *not* be with you than the sun could not be in one of its rays, or the ocean be absent from the waves that form and dissolve on its surface. I have made countless efforts to harness the universe to work on my behalf. None of those attempts got me anywhere until I realized that life was already doing everything it could to further my good. You don't have to tell the Force how to help you. You just have to let it find you and work for you and through you. A more accurate benediction would be, "May you be with the Force."

The Tao, which *is* the Force, is fully present, alive, and unassailable by the illusions that cloud our vision as we plod through a world of shadows and distortions. In spite of the shambles that human folly has made of life on earth, the Great Way stands intact, available to be used by all who recognize its power. Our dilemma is not that we do not have an invincible Source; our dilemma is that we do not realize It exists and we do not make use of It.

My words are easy to understand and easy to perform,

Yet no one under heaven knows them
or practices them.

My words have ancient beginnings.

My actions are disciplined.

Because people do not understand,
they have no knowledge of me.

Those that know me are few . . .

— 70

My purpose here is no mean goal. I intend to impart vision to the sightless; hope to the hopeless; passion to the numb; direction to the lost; and courage to the fearful. I can do this by pointing you within, where your answers live. *Tao Te Ching* affirms the majesty you own rather than requiring you to wrestle it from some external source. It reminds you that you already *are* what you seek. Thus ends lifetimes of searching for something outside to make you whole. When you remember you are perfect as creation intended, you have found the Tao, and the mystical marriage is consummated.

Distressed and confused, I went to see the master. I found him in his garden, pulling weeds from a section of Pu'er tea he had planted. Lao Tse did not see me approach, but he sensed my presence. "What's the matter?" he asked without even looking up.

"I just came from consulting the astrologer my mother recommended," I blurted. "He told me that I would have five years of bad luck. I am ready to throw myself off a bridge."

The master stood, wiped his hands clean of the soil, and faced me squarely. "So you are going to let an astrologer decide your future?"

"No, well, but . . . my mother has been seeing him for years. She swears by him. She hardly makes a decision without his approval. He is well respected in my city."

Lao Tse nodded. "I'm sure he is a good astrologer. But you have given your power away to him."

"So astrology is not valid?"

"All sciences are valid depending on how they are used. If they empower you to live more fully, they help. If they make you feel like a puppet on a string that someone else is pulling, they hurt. A knife can be used to heal through surgery or it can kill. It's all what you do with it."

Now I was more confused. "So I should disregard the astrologer's advice?"

"You should look within for your answers. Your life is not determined by the stars. It is determined by your state of mind and the choices you make. Regardless of how the stars are configured, you are in charge of your journey. Make healthy choices, and even if adversity comes, the Tao will show you how to use it for your benefit."

Lao Tse turned and returned to his weeding. When the master was done speaking, he was done speaking. The rest was up to me.

Five years have passed since that day. I am still here. I have had hard times and I have had easy times. I decided to meet the difficulties by asking how each situation can strengthen me. I am no longer afraid of adversity. As the master once told me, "What's in the way *is* the way."

If you knew who walks beside you on the path that you have chosen, fear would be impossible.

— A Course in Miracles

LET NATURE
TAKE ITS COURSE

The human being follows the earth.
Earth follows heaven.
Heaven follows the Tao.
Tao follows what is natural.
— 25

All of our dog expert friends told us that our nine-month-old male puppy was too young to mate with our older female. But he didn't get that memo. One night while my beloved Dee and I were sitting in our living room, we heard a sharp yelp from the kitchen. We rushed in to find the little guy stuck to the older woman. They remained interlocked for 45 minutes with a baffled look on their faces: "Now what do we do?"

Dee and I had the same question when, nine weeks later, we welcomed three tiny furball puppies into our family. We were going to give them away, but when the time came, we had fallen in love with all of them and could not imagine parting. "We can't have five dogs," we said. But we do. Our fur family has become a source of unspeakable joy, and our lives revolve around our "kids," with endless walks, play, cuddles, and frolics. I wouldn't trade being a dog dad for any other lifestyle. I saw a video prank in which an actor went to a dog park and offered people $100,000 and then $1,000,000 for their dog. Not one person accepted. You can't replace love with money.

The best things that happen are unplanned. The Tao has an idea of what wants to happen. Let it. While *Tao Te Ching*'s 5,000 characters are already quite succinct, we can boil the entire teaching down to five words:

Let nature take its course.

Sooner or later we must decide if nature is working *for* us or *against* us. Is life our enemy or our friend? While the world that people have manufactured is highly dysfunctional, is there a fundamental sanity beyond the chaos the five senses perceive? Was the world set up to work, and could it be working in spite of appearances? Is there a plan that includes the cycles of nature, yet transcends them?

Cultures on planet Earth have historically related to nature in one of three different ways: (1) man *under* nature; (2) man *over* nature; and (3) man *in* nature. "Man under nature" cultures are typified by ancient Greek, Roman, and Mayan civilizations, as well as some contemporary sects that believe the world is ruled by gods, demigods, and spirits superior to humanity. These elementals, we are told, chart our destiny, so we lower beings must bow down to them, appease them, make sacrifices, and, whatever you do, don't piss them off. Such cultures believe that favorable conditions are a boon from higher powers, and calamities are punishments for man's misdeeds.

Our technologically bullying culture is a staggering representation of the belief in "man over nature." We regard nature as our enemy to be overrun, or an obstacle to be mastered, controlled, and subjugated for our purposes. We tear down forests, dam rivers, preserve food with chemicals, manipulate genes, and spew toxins in the air with no awareness that when we hurt our planet, we hurt ourselves. Ancient gods have been replaced by the god of technology, our unflinching ally that provides weapons to conquer the universe at the touch of a button. But, as *Tao Te Ching* teaches, only what is of the Tao will endure.

"Nature bats last." We must honor what was created rather than attempting to override it.

The third model, "man in nature," is the only one that works, and the way we were born to live. Many cultures close to the earth understand that our purpose is to cooperate with nature, align with it, thank its Creator, discover the blessings it bestows, give back to it, and care for it. Native American, First Nation, Hawaiian, Aboriginal, and Maori cultures, among other indigenous peoples, recognize the crucial need to work *with* nature rather than control or hide from it. Such peoples' deep spirituality embraces respect for creation and seeks but to use it for the welfare of all.

The highest good is like water.

Water gives life to the ten thousand things and does not strive.

It flows in places people reject and so is like the Tao.

In dwelling, be close to the land.

In meditation, go deep in the heart.

— 8

The Gift of Redirection

The good news, which at first may seem bad but ultimately heals us, is that when we veer from nature it will move us (that's a gentle term for an often harsher experience) to find our way back. Such guidance can come easily if we are sensitive to the signs and we act on them, or it can come the hard way if we ignore or resist the messages. If we listen to the whisper, we don't need the slap. I saw a documentary about a French apple farmer who regularly sprayed his orchard with 19 different chemical pesticides. As a result of his exposure to these toxic materials, he developed a tick and began to have seizures. When he came to recognize the connection between the chemicals he was handling and his alarming symptoms, he switched to organic farming and his condition improved. His ill health was not a punishment. It was a wake-up call. Nature was saying, "The way you are approaching this is not in harmony with the Tao. Please heed the signs and make a correction so you can feel better and foster the well-being of the planet and the people you affect."

What messages from the Tao are you receiving to help you return to your natural state of wellness? What is your body telling you? Your job? Your relationships? Your financial world? What do you see in government, economics, health care, education, and business that represent nature's attempts to show us what is *not* the Great Way so we can reclaim our intended path? Nature is the clearest and most honest teacher in creation. We can fool each other, but not the natural world. Let us allow the natural world to teach us how to return to the Great Way with grace and ease rather than hardship.

Knowing harmony is constancy.

Knowing constancy is enlightenment.

It is not wise to rush about.

Trying to control the breath causes strain.

If too much energy is used, exhaustion follows.

This is not the way of Tao.

Whatever is contrary to Tao will not last long.

— 55

Rhythms and Cycles

Everything in nature functions in rhythms, waves, and cycles. Visionary scientist Nikola Tesla said, "If you want to find the secrets of the universe, think in terms of energy, frequency, and vibration." Every element of creation, from the tiniest atom to the farthest galaxy, is vibrating and cycling. To attempt to keep nature from taking its course is truly the impossible dream. *A Course in Miracles* tells us,

Your self-deceptions cannot take the place of truth.
No more than can a child who throws a stick into the ocean
change the coming and the going of the tides,
the warming of the water by the sun,
the silver of the moon on it by night.

We cannot defeat nature; if we really understood the genius behind the fabric of life, we would not want to. Why would we murder our best friend? It is the design by which the Creator has spun the universe into existence and placed us at the heart of creation, that we may be blessed and sustained by it. If we stand a chance of surviving and thriving, we must trust nature, find our place in it, and do what we can to further it, so it can further us.

While my friend Deborah was scuba diving off the coast of Monterey, California, she swam into a field of kelp that tangled around her until she was trapped. At first Deborah panicked and began to thrash about, trying to free herself. But the more she struggled, the more ensnared she became. Then she realized that the current had a pattern of moving the kelp in one direction, then the other, in an underwater dance. So Deborah began to move with the current and the kelp rather than fighting against them. When she aligned with the rhythm, she was able to work her way free.

Likewise there are waves and cycles in politics, the economy, business, and relationships. Politics are based on polarity, and the pendulum of leadership and policy swings back and forth. The economy has surges and dips. Real estate is hot, then cold, and then hot again. On a personal level, you may sometimes wish to be with people, while at other times you prefer to be alone. There is a time for work and a time for play. At one time I felt overwhelmed and I took a sabbatical in Fiji. I fantasized about strolling on secluded beaches for the rest of my life. At first my quiet time was soothing, the perfect respite after intense activity. After a while, I felt bored. I missed the elements of my work that I enjoy. Eventually I got back into work mode, renewed. I realized that I did not want to work all the time or play all the time. I enjoy the mix and the balance. Likewise, people who retire need something productive to do. You can't fill your golden years with golf alone. People who have nothing to do get bored or depressed, or die. We all need a purpose. We are here to do something as well as relax; to go out and then to go in. When you tap into that essential cycle, you walk the Great Way.

I sat beside my grandmother's bed, watching her body wither. How painful it was to see this once-vital woman shrivel to nearly nothing. The doctor said that he had done all he could do for her; now it was just a matter of time until she would be gone. I held Grandma's hand and looked into her glassy eyes. She turned her head on her pillow and offered a soft smile. She had always been so kind to me. It was hard to see her go.

I turned to my sister Biyu and took her hand. She, too, loved Grandmother, and I could see tears in her eyes. Biyu was very strong and I rarely saw her weep. But today she showed her tender heart. We were saying good-bye.

I looked down at Biyu's pregnant belly. It would be just two months now until her baby came. I wondered if perhaps Grandmother's spirit would return as her own great-granddaughter. I had heard of such things. I silently prayed that it might be so.

After the funeral, I went to see Lao Tse. "Why do people have to die?" I asked him.

The master stirred the embers in the fire slowly and then came to sit beside me. "It's just the way the world was set up," he told me. "When someone or something dies, that person or thing has played its part. It has no more purpose here. If it had a purpose, it would remain."

His answer didn't satisfy me. "Why can't we just live forever?"

He smiled, the glow of the fire falling softly on his weathered cheek. "We do. It is but the body that dies. Our true self lives on. What dies never really lived. The body is simply dust animated by spirit. The spirit is not confined to the body. We all live forever, I promise you."

That brought me some comfort to think that a part of my grandmother lived on, as we all might.

Lao Tse looked into my eyes intently. "The Tao calls you to trust comings and goings. Each occurs in its own right time and leads to the next step in the cycle. Life does not go in circles. It is constantly cycling upward. Let cycles play themselves out and they will reveal their purpose to you."

The master's answer made sense to my mind, but my heart was still aching over losing my grandmother. He sensed my disquiet.

"The heart knows the answers to the questions the mind cannot satisfy," he said. "Your grandmother is safe and loved, as you are."

When Lao Tse said that, a peace came over me. My mind still hungered, but my heart was filled. That was what I was yearning for.

The world is governed by letting things take their course.

It cannot be governed through interference.

—— 48

The Greatest Power at the Lightest Touch

When you act in harmony with the Tao, you gather the greatest power with the lightest touch. The hugely successful Women's March after the 2017 presidential inauguration demonstrates the power of the Tao. Teresa Shook, a grandmother and retiree living in the tiny remote town of Hana, Maui, thought that women should stand up for their rights in the face of a new administration unfavorable to the feminine. She posted a suggestion on her Facebook page, "I think we should march." Teresa pressed the *Post* button and went to sleep. The next morning she woke up and was astounded to find 10,000 "likes" in response! Enthusiasm for the march went viral, and when the day finally came, nearly three million women, men, and children marched in the United States—the largest single-day protest in U.S. history—along with millions of people in 63 countries on seven continents. If you knew how remote is the tiny village where Teresa lives, you would be even more amazed. To get there, you must drive a long and winding road for at least two hours and traverse 620 curves and 59 one-lane bridges. A small grocery store at the end of the trail sells T-shirts proclaiming, "I survived the road to Hana." From this obscure locale, with the touch of a button, a record-setting movement was born. Victor Hugo said, "Nothing is as powerful as an idea whose time has come." If your idea is aligned with the Tao, it will have a life of its own and it will reach all the right people in the right way at the perfect time. You will watch in awe as the river carries your boat to the ocean. When nature takes its course, there is no stopping it.

The valley spirit never dies;

It is the woman, primal mother.

Her gateway is the root of heaven and earth.

It is like a veil barely seen.

Use it; it will never fail.

— 6

Beyond Skyscrapers

When I present retreats in Hawaii for Japanese participants, one of the most common comments I hear is, "I didn't know there were so many stars! We don't see them in Tokyo." The statement is also a metaphor: When we build physical and psychological cities that obscure the stars, we must find our way to places that remind us of a Power greater than human architecture. The tallest buildings in the world, stunning and attractive as many are, cannot pierce the glory of the heavens. No matter how high our skyscrapers rise, there will always be uncountable stars beyond them.

A woman phoned my radio show and asked for advice on how to calm down her young hyperactive son. I asked her what she had noticed about ways to ground him. "He loves to be outside," she explained. "When I take him to a stream, he enjoys playing with rocks and sticks in the water. He can do this for hours." I reminded her that simply being in nature is healing. Her son knew what he had to do to feel balanced. The boy was his mother's teacher, guiding her to nature for her benefit as well as his. At a time when children from very young ages are becoming immersed and obsessed with electronic devices, as are many adults, regular doses of nature become our salvation. Lao Tse's advice, set forth nearly three millennia ago, is even more relevant today. Let us put his wisdom into practice, that we may restore ourselves and our planet to the natural order of life. When we do, we will remember why we are here, and creation will become our friend as it was in the beginning.

Stand before it and there is no beginning.

Follow it and there is no end.

Stay with the ancient Tao,

Move with the present.

Knowing the ancient beginning
is the essence of Tao.

— 14

QUIT
DOING GOOD

Not putting on a display,
[The wise] shine forth.
Not justifying themselves,
They are distinguished.
Not boasting,
They receive recognition.
Not bragging,
They never falter.
They do not quarrel,
So no one quarrels with them.
Therefore the ancients say, "Yield and overcome."
Is that an empty saying?
Be truly whole,
And all things will come to you.
—— 22

When a woman in the African Himba tribe knows she is pregnant, she goes into the wilderness with some friends, and together they pray and meditate until they hear the song of the child. The tribe believes that every human being has a unique energy that can be expressed as a song that represents that person's soul. The women then teach the song to the tribe, and when the baby is born, the villagers gather to sing the child into the world.

Then, at significant milestones in the child's life, such as the beginning of education, initiation to adulthood, marriage, and childbirth, the villagers sing that person his or her song. Finally, when that individual is ready to pass from this life, the tribe sings that person on to the next world.

There is one other time when the villagers sing that community member their song. If he or she commits a crime or socially unacceptable act, that person is called to the center of the village and the community sings the person's song. The tribe realizes that correction is achieved not by punishment, but by remembering who we truly are.

Lao Tse would agree that our true self knows how to live. When we live according to our nature, we don't need anyone else to prescribe our path for us. We know all we need to know from the inside out. Rules are for people who have lost touch with their inner guidance. Laws are also misused by unscrupulous leaders to control others for self-serving purposes. Lao Tse might say:

The more rules, the less freedom.

The less freedom, the less happiness.

The less happiness, the more crime.

The more crime, the more rules.

In a society of enlightened people, there would be no need for rules, laws, police, punishment, or prison. At any choice point, each person would consult his integrity and do what would maximally serve the individual and society. Every person would give according to her resources and take according to her need. In our society, however, many of us have become disconnected from our innate wisdom. We don't trust ourselves, so we depend on external authority to tell us how to live. It seems easier to obey than to think. We entrust our lives to government, religion, education, economics, medicine, culture, and family. If you removed your belief in what other people tell you about how you should live, you would have to fall back on your inner knowing. Could you do it?

Faith in internal guidance represents a defining leap in personal and planetary evolution. It is the severing of the umbilicus from dictatorship and dogma. While deep self-confidence seems like a foray into uncharted territory, it is really a homecoming. As the German philosopher Goethe said, "As soon as you trust yourself, you will know how to live."

Therefore truly great people dwell on what is real
and not what is on the surface,

On the fruit and not the flower.

— 38

Where Goodness Lives

You have been trained to believe that you are not good enough as you are. You are fundamentally flawed or lacking and there is something you need to do to become lovable and acceptable. You must become smarter, skinnier, younger, richer, sexier, married, and have children. You must impress your friends with the size of your engagement ring, enlarge your lips, hang more diplomas on your wall, garner more trophies, and display photos of yourself with important people. When I lived in Fiji, where most people have no money and a handful has a lot, a famous kava (ceremonial drink) dealer lived in a sprawling house beside a highway. He purchased a BMW Z4 sports car, tantamount to a Rolls-Royce in that country. Then he built an open-air showcase pavilion for it right beside the highway, with colored lights pointing at the vehicle from different angles. Everyone who drove past the car was reminded that this man is very rich and he can prove it. I never saw the car off the pavilion; I don't know that he ever drove it. It was a trophy. In our culture, we are generally not as ostentatious, but we do love to flaunt our toys. Yet what it takes to get and keep a sprawling storehouse of playthings is not so much fun. Some of us sweat for a lifetime on a treadmill of neurotically motivated achievement. But even as we add letters after our name and wings to our home, our heart still yearns for fulfillment that can come only from within.

Those who stand on tiptoe are not steady.
Those who stride cannot maintain the pace.
Those who put on a show are not enlightened.
Those who are self-righteous are not respected.
Those who boast achieve nothing.
Those who brag will not endure.
According to followers of the Tao,
"These are unnecessary food and baggage."
They do not bring happiness.
Therefore followers of the Tao avoid them.

— 24

A more subtle yet even more debilitating quest is to become a good person. Rather than seeking to wow other people with our looks or trophies, we seek to impress them with our personality, intelligence, or righteous actions. Gaining the respect and approval of others is the goal. If people think you are good, you win. But, Lao Tse would say, with this motivation you really lose.

Truly good people do nothing,
Yet leave nothing undone.
Foolish people are always doing,
Yet much remains to be done.

— 38

The goal to become a good person is ill-fated, because the quest is based on the false premise that you are not already good. When you proceed from a lie, you have to pile more and more lies upon it to keep the original lie going. So your quest is doomed before it even begins. All the good you attempt to do reinforces the belief that you are not good and you must fill a gap that doesn't exist. Consider the math parable of the "half-jumping frog." A frog leaps toward a goal, and he traverses half the remaining distance with each jump. The first jump takes him 50 percent there. The next jump moves him 50 percent of the remaining distance. And so on. When will the frog finally reach the goal? *Never.* The way he is jumping ensures he will never get there. When we seek unattainable goals, or goals that have already been reached, our efforts are fruitless. The way to reach a goal you already own is not to keep jumping halfway; it is to recognize you never needed to jump in the first place. Attempting to complete what is already whole creates a nonexistent split that can be healed only by recognizing that the split never occurred.

When I was studying with my mentor Hilda, a fellow student gave her a car. (My teacher never charged for her classes or healing sessions; she lived strictly on voluntary donations by appreciative students.) The student asked me to deliver the car to Hilda after our evening class in Manhattan. When I told Hilda I had the car for her, she replied, "Why don't you just keep it and bring it to me next week?" Eager to be recognized as the bearer of the gift, I didn't realize that my teacher was giving me a hint. "That's okay, Hilda, you can take it tonight," I replied. Again she suggested for me to wait, and again I rebuffed her plan. I wanted to be the good guy who delivered her the car that night. After another round of the same conversation, Hilda renounced her urging and said, "All right, then, I'll take it tonight."

I proudly gave my teacher the car keys and went down into the subway to find my way home. But, unfamiliar with the Manhattan subway system, I took the wrong train. Fifteen minutes later, I found myself at a station in the South Bronx late at night—a dangerous place during that era in New York. As I scanned the tough faces around the station, I dearly wished I had taken her advice and gone home with the car. I caught the first train in the opposite direction and eventually found my way back. But not before I learned a life-changing lesson in the importance of following The Plan rather than imposing my own will so I would appear the good guy.

Truly good people are not aware of their goodness,
And are therefore good.
Foolish people try to be good,
And are therefore not good.

—— 38

You need not and cannot attain goodness. You already own and are all the good you are striving to attain. Your intrinsic value is etched into your soul like light is an attribute of the sun. Neither can your value be compromised or lost because of anything you have done. No matter what the numbers on a scale show you, your drinking or drugging habit, your unspoken or acted-out sexual fantasies, your history of breakups or divorces, how much you have yelled at your kids, the money you snatched from the till, or the vast sum you paid for cosmetic surgery that you could have donated to charity, your soul remains intact. You are good not for what you do, but for who you are. When you recognize your deep inherent value, you make wise decisions that lead to greater good for you and everyone involved. Lao Tse would say, "Trust what you are, and all that you do will bless the world."

I was surprised to see Qi Zhuang at Lao Tse's door. The village spokesman had made the arduous hike up the mountainside to report that respected elder Ju Shang had died, and the community was taking up a collection for his widow.

Lao Tse greeted Qi Zhuang warmly and invited him in for tea. After a congenial conversation, the request for a donation came. Lao Tse went to his purse, removed a generous sum, and handed the coins to Qi Zhuang, who was quite grateful. "I am sure that the widow Shang will be very thankful for your gift," he said with a bow.

Lao Tse shook his head and lifted his hand in polite protest. "Please do not tell her this is from me," the master pleaded. "Tell her it is from an anonymous source."

"Why?" Qi Zhuang asked. "She will be honored that you contributed."

"I do not need such an honor. I would prefer that she consider that her gift came from the Tao."

"Very well," Qi Zhuang replied. "I shall respect your request." With that, he retrieved his hat and took his leave.

As soon as Lao Tse closed the door behind his guest, I asked the master why he refused to be associated with the donation.

"The quest for name, fame, and social acknowledgment is not the way of the Tao. People do all kinds of good things just so they will be publicly honored. They have their names engraved on plaques at temples, have buildings named after them, and swell with pride when the amount of their donation is announced. This is all vanity. The Tao gave them their money, and only the Tao should be recognized as the donor. My name is meaningless in the grand design of providence. We must give credit where credit is due, and not assume false origination."

Hearing that, I remembered that my father had once gotten into a nasty fight with a priest because the priest had given another man a more prestigious seat in the temple. My father argued that he had given a bigger donation to the temple than the other man. The priest replied that the other fellow was more pious in his devotion. My father left the temple in a huff and did not return again. After listening to Lao Tse's teaching, I realized that it was my father's pride that distanced him from the Tao. I made up my mind that if I ever had any money to give, I would give it anonymously, like the master.

Give up sainthood, renounce wisdom,
And it will be a hundred times better for everyone.
Give up kindness, renounce morality,
And people will rediscover filial piety and love.

—— 19

Fair or Powerful?

One of the ways we try to dole out morality is to make rules about the form goodness should take and what is fair. But there is more to fairness than meets the eye. Some friends of mine are a husband-and-wife team of ministers at a church. At the outset of their ministry, the two alternated delivering the sermon at Sunday services. On the Sundays when the wife, a very eloquent speaker, addressed the congregation, large numbers of people showed up. On the alternate Sundays when the husband spoke, about half the number of congregants attended.

When the couple became aware of the disparity in attendance, they decided that no matter how many people showed up, the fair thing to do was to continue to give each minister an equal opportunity to speak. But as time went on, the numbers of listeners to the wife increased, and the audiences for the husband decreased. The issue came to a head when the church began to face financial difficulties.

The couple revisited their agreement and realized that they were receiving a clear message: The wife was to be the Sunday speaker. Although the husband's ego was bruised, he admitted that he did not really enjoy speaking; there were other aspects of the ministry about which he was more passionate, such as working with the youth group. So the couple divided their responsibilities according to their personal strengths, enthusiasm, and the maximal results they could each manifest. The wife spoke on Sundays and the husband managed the youth program. Soon the Sunday attendance shot up consistently, the youth group attendance swelled, and the church stepped into unprecedented prosperity.

You cannot legislate or bureaucratize what is fair, because what is fair is unique to each circumstance. The ego, in its fundamental insecurity, seeks to make rules that apply in every situation. But a more mature understanding applies action according to need, not dogma. No act is always right or always wrong. If someone took a hatchet and broke into your house to steal something, it would be wrong. But if your house was on fire and a firefighter broke into your house with a hatchet to extinguish the fire, you would be grateful. If you wish to master the Tao, look within to discern appropriate action. Ultimately the way in is the way out.

> *When the great Tao is forgotten,*
>
> *Kindness and morality arise.*
>
> *When wisdom and intelligence are born,*
>
> *The great pretense begins.*
>
> —— 18

Rules, Laws, Illusions, and Truth

There is a crucial difference between universal laws and man-made rules. Universal laws are solid and eternal, the foundation upon which all creation rests. They function impeccably, and as we align with them they work in our favor. Some man-made laws are in harmony with the Tao, but many others distort or contradict it. Such rules are bendable and changeable, and people do not heed them because they are the product of human assumptions rather than invincible reality.

For example, governments have set speed limits on our highways. Yet hardly anyone abides by them. Most people drive 5 or 10 miles over the speed limit without consequence. If you drive at the speed limit, other drivers will pass you and flip you the universal sign of displeasure as they go by. So the speed limit is not a law. It is a rule. Most states also have laws prohibiting talking on a cell phone while driving. Yet many people do. If you can break it, it's not a law. Some states and countries have laws that prohibit certain sexual positions and acts. The *Saturday Night Live* television show presented a hilarious skit that showed a couple in bed under the covers, supposedly cavorting in various sexual positions. Then a group of Supreme Court justices in black robes entered the bedroom with clipboards and pens. They surrounded the bed and occasionally peeped under the covers to see what position the couple was in. "That's acceptable," said one justice. Moments later another declared, "That's not allowed." This evaluation went on for a while. The absurdity of such judgments was obvious. People make up rules about sex that have nothing to do with joy, connection, or the Tao. We twist, bend, distort, and obscure universal principles to suit our neurotic fears, whims, judgments, prejudices, and limiting beliefs. Then we project them onto others, until enforcement becomes a sham.

Religions have endless rules, some of which are in harmony with the Tao, and many of which are not. Orthodox Judaism prescribes 613 commandments a pious Jew must observe, down to the minutest detail of everyday life. Since no human being could possibly fulfill all of these commandments, and few even know them, adherents are assured to come up deficient. Certain Islamic priests and scholars, interpreting the Koran, declare that bestiality, pedophilia, necrophilia, and rape are permissible, and in some cases required. Unbelievable as these injunctions sound, these "authorities" tout such aberrations as the word of God. Such pundits do not, of course, represent the religion as a whole or the many sincere people who practice their faith with ethics. But such interpretations are accepted by some as law rather than the product of a warped mind. Lest we be tempted to point a finger of judgment at Islam, we must also look into our own Old Testament, where we find injunctions equally devoid of sensibility. In the books of Leviticus and Exodus, we are told that we are required by God to burn a bull on the altar as a sacrifice; avoid women during the "uncleanness" of their menstrual period; not approach the altar of God if we have a visual impairment; not trim the hair around our temples; not touch the skin of a dead pig; not plant two different crops in the same field; or wear garments made of two different kinds of thread. If a man works on the Sabbath, he must be put to death, and if another man marries both a woman and her mother, all three shall be burned to death. If all of these punishments sound heavy-handed, they are offset by the good news that we are permitted to own slaves and, if necessary, sell a daughter into slavery.

While the Bible contains the word of God, it also contains the words of man, many of which are steeped in fear and illusion. To believe that every single word in the Bible is the word of God, despite millennia of translation, editing, interpretation, and omission, represents a form of laziness in which we are unwilling to exercise our God-given faculty to discern truth from fabrication. It's easier to say, "It must all be true" than to figure out what is true and what is false. Many of the ideas in the Bible, Koran, and other sacred texts are indeed the word of God; they provide a holy guide to a rewarding life and a productive society. Many other ideas will make us crazy and tear the fabric of society if we attempt to practice them as we have been taught by mistaken interpreters. Thus Lao Tse calls us to dig in rather than lean out; to let ourselves be guided by internal wisdom rather than external opinion. This is the mark of a mature soul.

> *When there is no peace within the family,*
> *Filial piety and devotion arise.*
> *When the country is confused and in chaos,*
> *Loyal ministers appear.*
>
> —— 18

Spiritually Legal

A helpful question to ask yourself when you stand at an ethical crossroads is, "Is this spiritually legal?" No matter what human opinion or man-made laws dictate, what course of action will be the most helpful?

For example, it is considered unethical to fool someone into believing something that is not true. But what if a story you made up could heal someone? The documentary *(Dis)Honesty: The Truth About Lies* introduces a fellow who was a passenger on an airplane being rocked by severe turbulence. Suddenly a woman seated near him was overtaken by intense panic, crying and screaming that the airplane was going to crash and everyone was going to die. This fellow approached the distraught woman and told her, "I am an aeronautical engineer. You are flying on the safest airplane in the world." He comforted her that there was no way this airplane was going to crash. Hearing this, the terrified woman settled down and reclaimed a degree of composure. She told him, "Jesus sent you to me." But this man was not an aeronautical engineer and he had no idea how the airplane was constructed. His intention was simply to soothe the woman's anxiety, which he did. He broke a social injunction in order to help someone—as well as diminish the damaging effect she would exert on the other passengers—and it worked. Was he at fault? Philosophical essayist Robert Brault sums up the answer neatly: "Today I bent the truth to be kind, and I have no regret, for I am far surer of what is kind than I am of what is true."

When I posted the above story on my Facebook page, one reader commented, "We are all living in the stories we made up. Why not substitute a healing story for a frightening one?" This brings us to a crucial point about the new age/new thought philosophy that "you create your own reality." This is a half-truth. You do not have the power to create reality. Reality has already been created quite nicely, and you are not endowed with the right to tinker with it. Reality *is*, regardless of your opinion for or against it or the stories you make up about it. What you do have the power to create is *your experience* of reality. You can manufacture heaven or hell with your thoughts and live in that world as if it were real. But when you wake up from the dream your mind has fabricated, reality remains intact. *Tao Te Ching* tells us that ultimate reality is benevolent. *A Course in Miracles* underscores, "Only the creations of light are real. Everything else is your own nightmare." So if you are going to "create" a "reality," be sure to create one that matches what has already been created. Then the Tao will be at your back like a firm wind that powers sailors home to port after a long day at sea.

When you are clear on the purpose behind your act, you have the answer as to whether or not you should do it. Fear takes you down one path, and faith down another. I heard a funny story from a friend who was in Japan during a typhoon. The Japanese are an extremely obedient culture; the society is based on a strict code of ethics everyone is expected to obey. In olden times, if you committed a social faux pas, you would be required to fall on the sword. To this day the Japanese are strictly trained to follow all prescribed rules, under penalty of guilt, shame, or punishment.

During this typhoon, practically everyone had taken cover indoors and there wasn't any traffic on the street. My friend happened to still be outside, dashing for shelter from the oncoming gale-force winds. Along his way he encountered several Japanese people also making their way back to safety. When this small group came to a red light, they stood at the crosswalk, waiting for the light to turn green to cross the street. There was no traffic and their lives were in danger, but still they had to obey the rules and not be guilty of jaywalking!

This is a clear example of denying one's fundamental instinct in order to follow social rules. At that moment the regular rules were totally inappropriate. It was culturally illegal for them to cross against the red light, but spiritually legal for them to protect their lives.

Therefore when Tao is lost, there is goodness.
When goodness is lost, there is kindness.
When kindness is lost, there is justice.
When justice is lost, there is ritual.
Now ritual is the husk of faith and loyalty,
the beginning of confusion.

— 38

Societal rules serve at the base level of human evolution. They are intended to curb primitive instincts and keep unconscious people from hurting each other. Good idea, let's keep them. But some members of the tribe have outgrown savagery and are capable of self-government rather than depending on external guidance. When you are in your right mind, you don't need others to tell you how to live. The only thing more important than doing good is knowing *why* you are doing good. When that "why" proceeds from your inherent wisdom, you are impeccably guided. Quit *doing* good, and just *be* good. Then the good you seek will come *to* you because it is coming *through* you.

Insist on yourself; never imitate. Your own gift you can
present every moment with the cumulative force of a
whole life's cultivation;
but of the adopted talent of another you have only an
extemporaneous half possession.
That which each can do best, none
but his Maker can teach him.

— RALPH WALDO EMERSON

HOW EASY
CAN IT GET?

*When you have learned how to decide with God, all
decisions become as easy and as right as breathing.
There is no effort, and you will be led as gently as if
you were being carried down a quiet path in summer.*

— A COURSE IN MIRACLES

On your life's journey you have faced and overcome many
limiting beliefs. Yet there is one fundamental principle that can
change your entire life when you understand and master it. You
may still be burdened by the belief that your life must be difficult
and you must struggle for your good. You might even believe,
"If it's not hard I must not be doing it right. I must be cheat-
ing or missing something." Such debilitating ideas are so deeply
ingrained in so many people that hardly anyone questions them
and only a handful have chosen a lighter path instead. Yet Lao
Tse, the master of ease, would have you know that you need not
anxiously strive. Instead, you can allow all to be done for you
and through you.

Several years ago, Dee and I decided to sell our home and
move to another location that would give us more nature around
us, and space for our dogs to frolic outdoors. We found a property we loved and simultaneously received a modest offer on our
home. We were not thrilled with the offer, but since it would
enable us to purchase our new place, we accepted it. We made a

deal on the new property, contingent on the sale of our home, and everything was lining up.

Then our buyer backed out. Yikes! Now how would we complete the purchase of our new home? We phoned a friend who has been successful with real estate investments and asked for her advice. "How much do you need to complete your purchase?" she asked. We told her the very steep sum. In a heartbeat she replied, "I can lend that to you. Don't sell your house at a low price. Keep it on the market until you can make a better deal." We were floored. We weren't looking for money from our friend. We were just looking for direction. But the Tao had our back. (Someone gave me a coffee mug inscribed with the motto Relax. God is in charge. Here was a demonstration it is so.) We completed the purchase of our new home and within the following year, our original home sold for a price far higher than we would have received if we had made a desperate deal. We gladly paid our friend back and we are now enjoying our new residence.

When a step is aligned with your well-being and that of everyone involved, universal intelligence will make it happen. The Tao has your back.

I was with Lao Tse when he received the letter from the renowned sage Confucius inviting Lao Tse to meet with him. Confucius would be passing for one day through Luoyi, a city of temples in the province of Qin where Lao Tse lived. You can imagine my excitement when the master invited me to accompany him on this once-in-a-lifetime opportunity to witness the meeting of two of the greatest teachers of all time.

It was late fall when we set out on the three-day journey to Luoyi. The first two days of our travels were uneventful—good weather, well-trod roads, and no robbers by the wayside.

On the third day, snow began to fall. While we thought we might be seeing just a passing flurry, within the hour the snowfall became so thick that we could see no more than a few yards ahead on the road.

The master scanned the forest beside the road. "There is a small sheltered area in that thicket of trees," he pointed out. "Let's stop here and wait for the storm to pass."

I grew anxious. "If we stop here and the snow continues, we could get stuck and be delayed for days. Confucius will be waiting. If we miss this appointment we may never see him again. Maybe we should just push on."

Lao Tse surveyed the road, covered now with thickening snow. "If we try to force our way ahead, we will not make much progress. This shelter has appeared for a reason. Let us take advantage of the opportunity. Somehow everything will work out."

I couldn't believe Lao Tse would give up the auspicious meeting so easily. But I had learned not to argue against his intuition. He always seemed to have some good reason I could not see. So I quit murmuring and followed him to the roadside.

We spent half an hour dragging fallen branches to form a small shelter. How I wished we had departed one day earlier! We would have stayed ahead of the storm and been on time to meet Confucius. Now we might miss him entirely.

We made a small fire and broke out our few provisions. Just then a horse-drawn wagon was passing by on the road. The driver saw our fire and stopped. "Are you alright?" he called. When we explained our situation, he replied, "You shouldn't stay here overnight. You will catch cold and maybe die. Please come home with me and have a good night's sleep."

Lao Tse and I did not hesitate to accept his invitation. We hopped into the buggy and our rescuer, who introduced himself as Buwei, drove us to his house in a small village not far away. Buwei's wife Lihua welcomed us graciously and fed us a hot dinner. I felt so lucky to be saved from such a dismal situation!

After dinner, these kind people gave us a dry place to sleep and warm blankets. As I lay down, I shuddered to think about how little sleep I would have gotten with scant protection from the snowstorm and cold.

When I awoke the next morning, I was delighted to see the sun shining brightly. Horses and people had already passed on the main road, clearing the path. Exuberant, I told

Lao Tse, "Let's get an early start. We may still be able to catch Confucius before he leaves Luoyi."

But instead of gathering his gear, the master pointed toward Buwei chopping firewood in the yard. "Buwei is working hard. He has helped us so much, and now we can make his burden easier by giving him a hand with his firewood."

Again I grew frustrated. "But don't you want to meet Confucius? His invitation is the supreme honor."

Lao Tse set his hand on my shoulder. "No, my friend. Helping someone who helped us is the supreme honor. What's the use of sitting with a spiritual master if we deny our brother?"

After a few moments my angst subsided and again I surrendered. This is how it always was with Lao Tse. I would resist and then surrender. Question and then let go. Worry and then drop back into trust.

We helped Buwei chop and stack firewood, and then Lao Tse assisted Lihua to prepare lunch. By late morning I knew that Confucius had already come and gone from our meeting point, and I gave up all hope of seeing the eminent philosopher.

After lunch Buwei offered, "Let me drive you to Luoyi. It will take you another full day to get there on foot. My horses can make it in half that time. I can do some business while I am there."

Four hours later, as the sun was setting, we arrived at the inn where Confucius had been scheduled to stay. I asked the innkeeper if the spiritual leader had given any indication of where he had gone since his visit.

"Master Confucius arrived just an hour ago. He was also delayed by the storm. He instructed me to tell you that he is looking forward to meeting with Lao Tse this evening."

Stunned, I turned to the master. He did not seem surprised. Humbled, I remarked, "You were in tune with the Tao all along, weren't you?"

He smiled and replied, "The Tao is always working in our favor, even when it appears otherwise. When we trust that what is happening is helping us, we end up in our right place."

I considered the perfection of all the events that had unfolded and how we were impeccably cared for. I wondered why I had ever doubted.

Become the master of the universe without striving.
— 57

Beyond Resistance

Specific tasks do not create struggle. What makes a situation hard is the *struggle attitude* we bring to it. We resist a circumstance or believe it must be hard, and so it is. Not because struggle is required, but because our thoughts are powerful and we can create experiences by our belief.

If you resisted nothing, you would never feel like you were working. There are two ways to minimize resistance: (1) Don't engage in activities you detest; and (2) If you must do something you would prefer not to do, drop your resistance to it. This is the fastest route to cruise through your life with a minimum of stress or pain. While this goal may seem fantastic, we need but observe masters of their crafts who make apparently difficult tasks look easy.

One evening while perusing Netflix, Dee and I discovered a television series hosted by painter Bob Ross. We were astonished to watch this gentle artist create majestic, detailed nature paintings in the short space of a 28-minute show. "How does he do that?" we kept asking each other. I have never seen someone work so lightly to generate a product so stunning. Bob has developed a very simple technique that gets remarkable results. His effort is minimal and his product is maximal. Of course Bob went through a learning curve to get where he is; it did not come overnight. But the learning process was in itself rewarding, and at some point he emerged into a field of extraordinary ease.

Just because so many people are in pain, or your life has been so painful, does not mean that is the way it has to be. It just means that we have historically chosen to fight our way upstream rather than flow with the current. What we call history is largely the record of fear-based human choices moving contrary to the

Tao. But our history is not our destiny. At any moment we are free to make new choices and create a new destiny.

When faced with struggle, conflict, or difficulty, ask yourself,

If I were willing to let this be easier,
how would I be approaching this differently?

In some cases, the path of ease will move you to take a different course of action. In other cases, you may simply need to shift your attitude. One thing is certain: Sanding *with* the grain, rather than against it, will get you maximal results far more quickly and effectively.

In the universe the difficult things are done as
though they were easy.

In the universe great acts are made up of small deeds.

The wise do not attempt anything very big,

And thus achieve greatness.

——— 63

Against or For?

Does the injunction to drop resistance mean we are to lie down and let people do things that hurt us or others? Should we not resist war, child abuse, and diseases? Are we to resign ourselves and the world to pain and suffering? Not at all. The key to eradicating injustice is the attitude you hold in your quest. When you battle something, you empower the undesirable situation. Instead, hold foremost in your mind the result you would rather create. Fight *for* your valued goal instead of fighting *against* the situation you do not prefer. When Mother Teresa was invited to speak at an antiwar rally, she declined. She explained, "Fighting against war is another form of war. If this were a pro-peace rally, I would attend."

This is called marching without appearing to move,
Rolling up your sleeves without showing your arm,
Capturing the enemy without attacking,
Being armed without weapons.

——— 69

If something comes up that you wish would go away, accept that it has come for a reason and consider how you can benefit from the experience. How is this situation stimulating you to grow in ways that you would not have grown had it not come forth? Is there an unseen opportunity here? Are you being guided to make a course correction that will ultimately improve your life? Every difficulty comes with a gift in its hands. It remains a problem until you accept the gift. Upon receiving the gift, the situation is transformed and it may resolve easily or even miraculously. Do your best to hold challenges in a higher light and do not lose sight of the many blessings in your life. The challenge occupies but a sector of your experience. There is much more to your life than this situation. Balance your efforts to handle this situation with soul-nurturing activities and fulfilling moments with people you love. Life is more a matter of perspective than facts. Align with the highest perspective, and the facts will take care of themselves or you will be precisely guided how to handle them.

The Tao of heaven does not strive and
yet it overcomes.
It does not speak and yet is answered.
It does not ask, yet all its needs are met.
It seems to have no aim and yet its
purpose is fulfilled.

——— 73

The End of Work

Following the path of ease does not mean that you run from difficulties. You may step into a challenging project, career path, or relationship. Your task may require time, effort, and perseverance. You may encounter roadblocks, uncooperative people, and apparent dead ends. But if you burn with the fire of purpose, your higher intention will gobble up the challenges. Setbacks will not bring you down, but propel you forward. It is said, "Choose a job you love and you will never work another day in your life."

When I write a book, for example, I am at my computer for many hours, sometimes long into the night. I become preoccupied with the material. I go over every sentence with a fine-tooth comb and I do scores of rewrites. To an observer it would appear that I am working hard. On one level I am, but on a deeper level I am working easy. My time is soul fulfilling and the hard parts are not debilitating, but empowering. The process is a lot more fun than difficult.

When I present an intensive weeklong seminar, I dig in with the participants and work with them to overcome their fears and blocks. Some of the stories and experiences participants recount are unspeakably horrid. Child physical and sexual abuse, satanic torture, rape, brutal war crimes, suicides of loved ones, and grisly events that spring from the darkest, basest, most sordid elements of the human condition. To work with these people and help them requires tremendous compassion and focus. Other clients are heavily resistant and I need a jackhammer to penetrate their thick armor. Some observers comment, "I can't believe you delve into such morbid psychic dungeons. It would drive me crazy to do that." But that is not my experience at all. I find the process deeply rewarding. I love forging past the suffering to come out on the other side and find healing. It is a holy opportunity to disperse the darkness with light. I have no resistance to this work, so it is not stressful for me. I find it exhilarating. By the end of the week, I am not tired at all. I have more energy than when I began.

By contrast, when I sit down with my company's accountant to go over our books, a few minutes seems too long. He tries to explain double-entry accounting to me, and I tell him, "I don't really understand this. That's why I hired you." He laughs and answers, "I love this! I can do it all day long!" He is in his right place and I am in mine. That's how the universe is designed to work. Life becomes difficult when you attempt to do things that don't belong to you. It becomes easy when you do what belongs to you. In these last two sentences you just read the cheat sheet for the entire *Tao Te Ching*.

> *Allow your life to unfold naturally.*
> *Know that it too is a vessel of perfection.*
> — 29

Dismounting the Four Horsemen

The belief in the requirement of suffering and the expectation of catastrophe is established by the ego at the personal level and projected onto the broader screen of the world. Just as we may be tempted to believe we are doomed as individuals, we may believe we are doomed as a world. Thus we are inundated with endless prophecies of world disaster. Disasters do happen, but well-being is far more pervasive. To escape from disaster, you must first escape from disaster consciousness. Extricate yourself from the dank bunker of anxious self-protection, and step into the sunlight of creative vision. If there is something you can do to offset adversity, do it. But do not give your power away to fear. Align with the presence of grace, and "surely goodness and mercy will follow me all the days of my life."

We are told in the book of Revelation about the prophesied Apocalypse, heralded by four symbolic horsemen, generally considered to be war, famine, death, and the Antichrist. Many people shudder to consider the coming of such a catastrophic epoch. What they do not realize is that the Apocalypse has been around for a long time. It is nothing new. The history of humanity has been plagued by war, famine, death, and deluded egocentric Antichrists. You don't need to worry about the Apocalypse coming. Been there, done that, bought the T-shirt. Instead, put the Apocalypse behind you and step into the postapocalyptic age. Humanity has suffered enough, and so have you. More suffering will not buy us more salvation. Pain hasn't freed us by now, and it will not do so anytime soon, or ever. If pain could buy salvation, we would all have been liberated a long time ago.

Lao Tse gives us the secret to finally finish the Apocalypse and live free of the terror it has wrought. He recorded his map out of hell 2,500 years ago, but humanity is a slow learner. Until now. If you are reading these words, it means that on some level you are ready to lighten up and walk the Great Way. You are free to hang out in the Apocalypse if you choose, but, to riff on a maxim, "5,000 words to the wise are sufficient."

The word *apocalypse* means "the lifting of the curtain." That curtain is the veil of illusion that makes it appear that we are separated from love. Such a condition is impossible, since the Tao is always present and it does not depend on our awareness of it to be so. Erroneous beliefs can create all kinds of experiences unlike reality, but they cannot replace it. When we wake up from the nightmare, or the curtain is lifted, we see reality as it is. Lao Tse assures us that reality supports us. It is only in the murky corridors of the fearful mind that things seem to have gone awry. Painful events are not a punishment or our destiny. They are an alarm clock waking us to return to the kindly universe we have turned our backs on, and claim the well-being we deserve.

Tao in the world is like a river flowing home to the sea.

— 32

Lao Tse in You

We can use the life of Lao Tse as a metaphor for our own spiritual journey. He is a symbolic figure as well as a historical one. Even if Lao Tse did not exist as a person, his story ushers us to the Great Way. Let us take a moment to revisit Lao Tse's odyssey as a reflection of our own. At one time the master held a high position as the dynasty's librarian in the bustling capital city of China, where he worked at the heart of the government and rubbed shoulders with rich and powerful people. Then he got fed up with political corruption and moral deterioration, and decided to leave so he could dwell closer to nature.

Likewise, many of us live in physical or psychological cities enmeshed in fear, competition, and ego-driven pursuits. At some point we realize that the life that most people are living, including our own, has drifted shockingly far from the Tao. We wake up one day and say, "I can't believe I've been living like this. There must be a better way." We yearn to return to our original innocence and leave behind the crazy, complicated, cruel world. Also like Lao Tse, we may be steeped in the "rewards" of the world, including materialistic possessions that promise to make our life easier, but effectively enslave us. We may hold a coveted position in the corporate world, academia, religion, entertainment, government, or the community. Then we recognize the emptiness of the goals we have striven for, and we yearn for a more soulful existence. Like the disgruntled newscaster Howard Beale in the classic film *Network*, we symbolically stick our head out of our office window and yell, "I'm mad as hell and I'm not gonna take it anymore!" Or depressed as hell, lonely, fearful, or powerless. Such abysmal alienation moves us to muster the courage to escape our castle-become-prison and, despite the fact that others regard us as insane or exert intense pressure to keep us in the fold, we exit the turmoil of the city and head homeward toward the world the Creator has established rather than the one distorted by man.

Fame or self: Which matters more?

Self or wealth: Which is more precious?

Gain or loss: Which causes more pain?

Those who are attached to things will suffer greatly.

Those who save will suffer heavy losses.

Those who are contented are never disappointed.

— 44

As Lao Tse was about to cross the western border en route to a simpler existence, a guard recognized him and begged him to record his wisdom as a legacy for those who followed. It was then that he penned the terse but penetrating 81 stanzas that have crept into the hearts of truth seekers for 25 centuries. Likewise, as you ascend to higher levels of consciousness, you are called to leave a gift for those also seeking to escape from suffering. Because you have experienced the aching separation from the Tao and chosen to reclaim the Great Way, your process of transformation is a priceless teaching for those who follow in your footsteps. You cannot leave selfishly. You must turn your departure into a blessing.

When we grow intolerant of social and political madness and we reach for a simpler, easier, saner life, we encounter dragons at the door of the temple, threatening to devour us with guilt for not suffering as we should. Or for choosing ease while others yet choose pain. In a culture that worships at the altar of sacrifice, the lighter pathway seems radical, even heretical. Yoga lifestyle teacher Rachel Brathen noted, "In a society that profits from your self-doubt, liking yourself is a rebellious act." Those still committed to suffering will argue, chastise, or reject you if you step out of the fray in favor of a freer journey. But the spiritual path is not a popularity contest or a democracy. The number of people who adopt a certain way of life does not make it right or justify it to be imposed on everyone. A herd mentality is a carryover from a more primitive level of evolution, and has no place in a society of conscious individuals. As we face our own fear or the resistance of others, we may be tempted to retreat to the familiar but painful world. Yet we can choose to step ahead anyway. Eventually there comes a crucial moment when the hardship of staying outweighs the fear of leaving. Then we finally do what we could have done a long time ago. When we miss the Tao enough, we will return to it.

> *Therefore the wise, traveling all day,*
> *Do not lose sight of their baggage.*
> *Though there are beautiful things to be seen,*
> *They remain unattached and calm.*
>
> — 26

Like Lao Tse, we are all destined to escape the polluted city and breathe fresher air. We will leave behind the suffocating world and pass through the portal to the land beyond the western wall. In ancient Egypt when someone passed away, those who survived him did not say he died. They said he "wested," meaning that, like the sun dips below the western horizon at the end of the day, that person simply faded out of sight, not to be seen again today, but surely to return tomorrow. Physical death is symbolic of the transition from one state of being to another. We all "die" many times during a lifetime when we leave behind what no longer serves us and we embrace what naturally comes next.

The journey from the mire to the mountaintop is well marked by those who have walked it before us. Like Jesus, Buddha, Muhammad, and other enlightened beings, Lao Tse found his way to higher ground and lingers at the gate for a while as a wayshower for we who follow. One day we shall all sit down to tea with the old master and laugh as we recount the winding path we took. We can hasten that momentous day by allowing this day to be easier than we once expected.

Blunt the sharpness,
Untangle the knot,
Soften the glare,
Merge with dust.
Oh, hidden deep but ever present!

—— 4

HOW TO
FIX THE WORLD

The softest thing in the universe

Overcomes the hardest thing in the universe.

*That without substance can enter where
there is no room.*

Hence I know the value of non-action.

Teaching without words and working without doing

Are understood by very few.

—— *43*

While Lao Tse and I were traveling through remote Quan-rong, evening fell and we found our way to an inn in a small village. Before retiring we went to the inn's tavern for dinner. There, a burly middle-aged man seated near us kept asking the waitress to refill his glass of *baijiu* until he became quite drunk. Then he began to insult the waitress in a loud voice.

Hearing the man's rudeness, a strapping young man seated nearby ordered the loudmouth to shut up. The drunk stood and an argument ensued until the older fellow called the other man horrible names. The young man grew red-faced and squared off to clout the oaf.

At the crucial moment Lao Tse stepped between the two and told the young man, "Please let me handle this." He turned to the drunk and asked in a soft voice, "Why, my friend, are you drowning yourself in *baijiu* tonight?"

The fellow calmed down a bit and said in a slur, "Ji is gone." He started to wobble, but then grabbed his chair to steady himself. Lao Tse placed a firming hand at his back. "Thirty-three years we were together," the man said bitterly. "Then she got sick and died—just like that," he said, banging the table with his hand, almost losing his balance. Lao Tse helped him sit down.

"What the hell is this damned life all about?" he ranted. "She was a good woman, my best friend. Now she's gone." A tear formed at the corner of the man's eye, which quickly gave way to more. The man stretched his arm on the table, let his head fall into the crook of his elbow, and began sobbing.

Lao Tse motioned for the innkeeper, who had been watching the incident. "Give this man a room for the night," the master said. "I will pay for his lodging and dinner."

Hearing these words, the man looked up at Lao Tse with puppy-dog eyes. He sniffled and wiped the tears off his cheeks. He took Lao Tse's hand and kissed it. "Thank you for your kindness. You don't know how hard it has been without her."

Lao Tse offered a sad smile. "I do know . . . Now get to bed and have a good night's sleep."

Mercy brings victory in battle and strength in defense.
It is the means by which heaven saves and guards.

— 67

We all feel the pain of the world. We wish we could take away the suffering we see. But it is all too much for any one person to undo. Despite our efforts and good intentions, sorrow, pain, and poverty seem overwhelming. Misery has endless company. The media streams a constant blare of war, disaster, crime, and death. People we talk to are negative and many feel defeated. Some struggle with physical hardships; others, financial stress; and others, turbulent relationships. How can we possibly help these people or change the world, beginning with our own?

Lao Tse tells us that real change proceeds from the inside out. Surface changes do not get to the core; only when we address the source of our problems do we heal their manifestations. My German client Ilsa told me that her daughter Greta went through a traumatic childhood. When Greta was a pre-teen, her father was killed in a car crash on the autobahn late at night. A few years later Ilsa remarried, and her new husband's teenage son began to sexually abuse Greta. He would regularly sneak into her bedroom while she was sleeping and molest her. As a result of these traumatic experiences, Greta registered a subconscious belief that bad things happen at night. She could not sleep, an issue that persisted into her young adulthood. A doctor prescribed sleeping pills to help Greta rest at night, but she was still drowsy during the day, so the doctor prescribed an amphetamine to keep her stimulated. These competing medications took a heavy toll on her body and psyche. Greta got together with a boyfriend she met in prep school in Switzerland, but, due to her history of molestation, had difficulties expressing herself sexually.

Around that time Ilsa attended a lecture in Munich on the Hawaiian healing technique of *ho'oponopono*, based on forgiveness and release. Ilsa passed the technique along to Greta, who welcomed it and applied it to her father, whom she resented for dying when she was so young, and to her stepbrother for his sexual abuse. Eventually Greta succeeded in forgiving both, and grew beyond the belief that bad things happen at night. She got off the medications and accepted her boyfriend's marriage proposal. When the time came for her outdoor wedding in the Alps, Greta needed someone to walk her down the aisle, but by that time her mom had divorced her second husband. So Greta asked her stepbrother, the very one who had molested her but whom by now she had forgiven. She now has a happy marriage and is doing well in her life.

This story illustrates two key principles underlying sustained healing: (1) Real transformation occurs not simply by manipulating the symptoms, but by going to the core and addressing the fear, pain, and beliefs that are causing the symptoms; and

(2) Healing occurs through release or forgiveness. Forgiveness does not mean that we condone abuse or cruelty. To the contrary, it means that we love ourselves enough to not accept negative behaviors directed at us. We further honor ourselves by deciding that letting go of the past will bring us greater benefit than holding onto it. When we can drop grievances and step fully into the present moment, we are free.

Stillness and tranquility restore order in the universe.

— 45

Why We Wish for Others to Change

There are two reasons you might seek to change another person's behavior: (1) They are annoying you in some way, and you believe that if they stopped doing what they are doing, you would feel better; or (2) They are in pain, you genuinely care about them, and you wish to help them find their way to higher ground. While these reasons appear to be different, they are essentially the same, since in both cases you believe you need someone else to change before you can be happy. But we can look at each scenario separately to build your skill sets to deal with them.

Achieving Correction

The list of ways that others bother us is endless. We observe parents, spouses, children, family members, friends, business associates, companies, governments, and cultures intruding on our happiness, and we wish they were different. "If only my husband would listen to me." "If only my wife would quit nagging me." "If only my kids would do better in school." "If only my boss would get off my case." "If only more people would buy my product." "If only my political party were in power." If only, if only, if only . . .

I ask my seminar audiences, "How many of you have tried to change someone else so their behavior will make you happier?" Most of the people in the audience raise their hands. Then I ask, "How many of you have succeeded?" Never has one person out of thousands raised their hand. The goal of changing other people to make you happy is fruitless. Get over it. You may be able to nag or intimidate someone to change, but inwardly the other person will resent you and look for ways to rebel, sabotage, or leave. Forced change is not true change; a backlash always follows. "A man convinced against his will is of the same opinion still." You know how awful it feels when someone else tries to change you to suit their desires. Why would you expect anyone else to accede when you attempt to impose your will on them?

My friend Diane was regularly irked by her husband Jerry's habit of making toast in the morning and leaving crumbs on the kitchen counter. Many times she asked Jerry to clean up the crumbs, but her requests didn't change his behavior. One morning Diane again found crumbs and started to complain in her mind. Then she considered, *The only thing worse than coming into the kitchen and finding crumbs would be to come into the kitchen and not find Jerry.* Diane realized that crumbs in the kitchen were a very minor issue in light of the deep love she felt for her partner. That was the end of the crumb problem for Diane and the beginning of peace of mind.

Sometimes you can change the environment. Always you can change your mind. If you can change your environment from a sense of positive vision, you will succeed. Remember to work *toward* what you want rather than *against* what you resist. All metaphysical teachings tell us that the world we see is a projection of the thoughts we are holding about it. To attempt to change the world without changing your mind is tantamount to making a run on the screen in a movie theater and trying to force the images to do something different. If you want to see a different movie, you must change the film in the projector. The film is your thoughts. The screen is the world. Insert a new film, and everything you see on the screen will be different.

Then it is best not to interfere.
If nothing is done, then all will be well.

—— 3

How to Be Truly Helpful

What if you sincerely care about someone who is struggling and you wish to help that person? Perhaps someone close to you has a drinking problem or other addiction; or is working to the point of illness; or is depressed or suicidal; or is doing something illegal that could get him in trouble; or is hurting other people? Your desire to change that person does not spring from selfish motives, for you genuinely value that person's happiness and you want them to choose better. According to Lao Tse's teaching of nondoing, are you supposed to just do nothing, stand by, and watch this person ruin their life?

Not at all. There is a way to help without imposing your will. Surrendering to the Great Way means allowing it to work *through* you, as well as around you. The Tao is doing the work, not you. If you feel moved to offer a listening ear, guidance, money, a home, gift, job, book, seminar, teacher, or any other form of support, please do so. Give what you can where you can, with a kind and generous heart. But do not be attached to the recipient changing because of your input. What the receiver does with your service is up to him or her. Here is where Lao Tse's notion of nondoing can save you a great deal of angst. You are not responsible to make a particular result happen. Truth be told, you have no idea what the other person requires for their highest good. Perhaps they will accept your offering, be grateful, and go on to live a happier life. Perhaps they will take a bit of your help and no more. Perhaps there is another form of help that will support them more. Perhaps they have to work with their situation more to glean a deeper lesson, rather than you rescuing them. Perhaps timing is a factor, and other elements must line up on your friend's behalf. There are many different ways this person may benefit and advance, only some of which you might be aware of, none of which you can be sure are the real answer. This is where humility and surrender, two of the essential teachings of *Tao Te Ching*, come into play. Do what you can with a whole heart, and then place that person you care about in the healing hands of the Tao.

Tao abides in non-action,

Yet nothing is left undone.

— 37

Ultimate Self-Protection

Think of someone you know who is just an awful person. This individual is mean-spirited, nasty, self-centered, narcissistic, and perhaps delusional. Maybe even pathological. Or perhaps you know someone who has severe mood swings, attempts to manipulate you, or plays games with your emotions that leave you feeling tattered and confused. You ask yourself, "How can I protect myself from their dark influence?"

The answer is simple, but requires understanding and practice. Don't meet this person on their terms. Refuse to enter the musty cave of illusions where they dwell. Stand firmly in the light. Maintain your dignity, peace, and clarity, no matter what that person does. When she goes low, you go high. Reframe your vision of this person as a friend who has come to help you tap into your soul and build spiritual muscles you would not have developed had your relationship been easier. You have "hired" this person to help you advance. Fighting this person, attacking, or dwelling on the injury they have caused will not get you what you want. This tactic has not succeeded thus far, and it will not start succeeding now. Only changing the way you see this person and the situation will get you out of hell. Anything else will just keep you spinning your wheels. Hold the high watch and you will graduate from the lesson they came to help you master. Then you will not need the challenge anymore and that person will either disappear from your world or will no longer disturb you.

> *Approach the universe with Tao,*
> *And evil will have no power.*
> *Not that evil is not powerful,*
> *But its power will not be used to harm others.*
> *Not only will it do no harm to others,*
> *But the wise will also be protected.*
>
> —— 60

The courage the Tao calls you to summon is not to conquer a person or nation, but to conquer the beliefs that suck joy from your life. It may seem easier to point your knife at other people rather than use it as a scalpel to dig out the venomous thoughts and feelings that have poisoned your well-being. People who attack others do so only to avoid facing and mastering their own lives. The sage, by contrast, realizes that self-mastery is the goal of life, and controlling, bullying, or needing to fix others is a distraction from our true purpose.

Someone who is mean and manipulative is steeped in fear, the densest of energies. When you grow fearful, upset, angry, or resistant, you match the negative frequency of the person you dislike. You are locked into a painful cycle by energetic agreement. You have no hope of escaping their influence because you are operating at precisely the same frequency.

When you choose a higher frequency, you rise above the denser energy. When an airplane encounters turbulent weather, the pilot raises the altitude of the craft to establish it in calmer skies. When you remain founded in your calm center, negativity cannot touch you because there is nothing in you that matches it. If you want someone to change, model the energy and behavior you wish that person would exhibit. Then you will achieve two crucial goals: (1) You will establish yourself in the strongest position to influence the other person to act uprightly; and (2) You will find the inner satisfaction you sought by attempting to change the other person.

> *If people are bad, do not abandon them . . .*
>
> *But remain still and offer the Tao.*
>
> *Why does everyone value the Tao?*
>
> *Isn't it because you find what you seek and are forgiven when you sin?*
>
> *Therefore this is the greatest treasure in the universe.*
>
> —— 62

Emmet Fox said,

> *There is no difficulty that enough love will not conquer: no disease that love will not heal: no door that enough love will not open . . . It makes no difference how deep set the trouble: how hopeless the outlook: how muddled the tangle: how great the mistake. A sufficient realization of love will dissolve it all. If only you could love enough you would be the happiest and most powerful being in the world . . .*

Tao Te Ching is all about empowerment. Not the kind of power the world strives for, but the sword of invincible truth that cuts through the entanglements spun by fear and carves a pathway to miracles. The Tao will accomplish everything for you that you cannot do for yourself. Jesus said, "I of myself can do nothing. It is the Father within me that does the work." *Father* equals Tao. That power, by whatever name you call it, will achieve all the correction you seek for yourself and others. The world is not as solid as you have been taught. It changes as you change your mind about it. Just get out of the way and let the Tao fix what was never broken.

Those who know how to live walk abroad

Without fear of rhinoceroses or tigers.

They will not be wounded in battle.

For in them the rhinoceros finds no place to
thrust its horn,

Nor the tiger to use its claws,

And weapons no place to pierce.

Why is this?

Because they have no place for death to enter.

—— 50

HUMBLED
AND EXALTED

I have three treasures which I hold and keep.

The first is mercy; the second is economy;

The third is daring not to be ahead of others.

From mercy comes courage; from economy
comes generosity;

From humility comes leadership.

—— 67

Akoni Pule was a statesman of Japanese descent who was elected to the Hawaii State House of Representatives in 1947. He served for two years and then he was defeated for reelection. Then Akoni Pule did something hardly anyone would do. He took a job as a janitor in the congress building so he could stay in the environment of politics and learn more about how the legislature worked. It must have been very humbling for Mr. Pule to mop the floor behind the man who defeated him.

Two years later, Pule ran for office again, he was elected, and he went on to serve continuously from 1952 until 1965—one of the longest runs in the history of the state. During that time he championed the cause of native Hawaiians, instituted a thriving seaport, and became a highly respected leader. After a 10-year campaign to build a road that allowed residents in a remote area to get to jobs at a new hotel, the highway was named after him.

If you would guide the people, you must
serve with humility.

If you would lead them, you must follow behind.

In this way when you rule, the people will
not feel oppressed;

When you stand before them, they will not be harmed.

The whole world will support you and
will not tire of you.

— 66

Humility is the most consistent trait identified in *Tao Te Ching* as the doorway to fulfillment and success. Lao Tse underscores this noble virtue 59 times in his 81 stanzas. Humility calls us to disavow the tyranny of ego-driven striving and allow our lives to be guided and protected by the Tao. The Bible tells us, "He who humbles himself shall be exalted." The Talmud echoes, "He who seeks reputation shall lose it. He who does not seek reputation shall gain it." The plot to gain name, fame, and worldly power always fails because it is misaligned with the Tao, which, properly harnessed, affords us the strength of the entire universe. If you are to be rich, powerful, and in the public eye because the Tao puts you there, you will succeed and be at peace. If you seek such position by your own devices, you will fail miserably. You might achieve your worldly goals, but without the proper motivation, your soul will be shredded. Strive to live in alignment with the Tao's kindly will for you, and you will succeed without struggle and enjoy the peace your soul seeks.

One morning at the market, the master bought a large bag of lychees, his favorite fruit. He gave the vendor, a frail older man with one blind eye, a bronze coin, greater in value than the price of the fruit. The vendor took the coin and wished the master a good day.

"Excuse me, sir," the master said, "do you have some change for me?"

The vendor shook his head. "No, you gave me a copper coin equal to the price of the lychees."

"I do not wish to argue, but I gave you a bronze coin."

The man shook his head. "It was copper."

I began to feel incensed. "I saw the coin," I interjected. "You owe him change."

The master put his hand on my arm, as if to advise me to be quiet. He thought for a moment and told the vendor, "Perhaps you are correct. Sorry, my mistake. Have a good day." With that, Lao Tse bowed and we continued along the street.

"But you did give him a larger coin, and you deserve change," I said, annoyed. "That was very petty of the vendor to argue with you over such a small amount of money."

"Yes, but it would have been just as petty for me to argue with him over it. Even if it were a larger sum, money is not worth arguing over. People use money as an excuse to play out their fears of lack. If they knew they lived in an abundant universe, they would know that their needs are always supplied."

Then it occurred to me that I never saw the master engage in any conflicts over money. "If I wanted to pit myself against that man, we would still be there arguing," he added. "But instead I am free to enjoy my day. That money will come back in some other way. I am not concerned about it."

As we approached another stand, I asked, "Do you think the vendor made a mistake because he is blind in one eye?"

"We are all blind in one eye," the master replied. "For that reason we need to let our decisions be guided by the eye that can see."

A Tale of Two Managers

Be not deceived by ups and downs that occur in the short run, or appearances of disorder. No matter what evil or error seems to rule, truth eventually makes itself known, character is revealed, and virtue prevails.

When I needed to hire a business manager, two applicants rose to the top of the field of candidates. The younger fellow, Mel, was enthusiastic but inexperienced. The other, Jack, was a mature man with a track record of success. I decided to hire the more experienced candidate. Mel was disappointed, but he told me that if I had any projects for him, he would be happy to work on them. I gave him one project. After a few months with Jack at the helm, I found that his motivation was sorely lacking and he did such a poor job that the business was faltering. I clearly needed to let him go. Meanwhile, Mel had performed in exemplary fashion on his one project, so I hired him to guide the business. He did an outstanding job and we worked together for seven years, during which the company prospered and spilt its blessing to both Mel and me.

If Mel had slipped into ego and become insulted or angry because he was not awarded the position, he would have missed out on a great opportunity. But his humility and willingness to serve set him up for success. When everything shook down, he was the perfect person for the position and the Tao (which some might call in today's terms "the law of attraction") rearranged everything to the highest benefit.

Therefore, those desiring a position
above others must speak humbly.
Those desiring to lead must follow.
— 66

Every event offers us a blank canvas upon which we paint with the brush of humility or arrogance; modesty or pride; service or self-aggrandizement. If we seek praise and position, we shall crash. If we seek character and service, we shall soar. Even if you do not have a highway named after you or you are not awarded the coveted job or prize, you will be at peace with yourself and your soul will be satisfied.

The flexible are preserved unbroken.
The bent become straight.
The empty are filled.
The exhausted become renewed.
The poor are enriched.
The rich are confounded . . .
The old saying that the flexible are preserved
unbroken is surely right!
If you have truly attained wholeness,
everything will flock to you.

— 22

WHEN A LITTLE
BECOMES A LOT

Without form there is no desire.
Without desire there is tranquillity.
And in this way all things would be at peace.
— 37

There is a scene in the classic movie *It's a Wonderful Life* in which bank manager George Bailey must contend with a panic-driven run on the bank. Fearful townspeople are lined up to withdraw their savings, which would break the bank if it had to pay out to everyone. When one fellow asks to withdraw all of his savings, George asks him, "How much do you really need?" The man thinks for a moment and responds with a number far smaller than his original demand. This act of sincerity sets in motion a wave of sanity that calms the other customers and moves them to ask for their actual need rather than an anxiety-driven sum. As a result, the bank is saved and everyone is able to get what they need.

The question, "What do you really need?" is the meditation of a lifetime. If you can distinguish between what you *think* you need and what you *really* need, you will realize that your true needs are far less than you have been taught, and you are always provided for.

Must I fear what others fear? What nonsense!
Everyone else is busy,
But I alone am aimless and without desire.
I am different.
I am nourished by the great mother.
— 20

I saw a bumper sticker that could have been composed by Lao Tse if he lived today:

The more you know, the less you need.

Need implies lack, a condition *Tao Te Ching* assures us does not exist.

While others rush about to get things done,
I accept what is offered.
I alone seem foolish, earning little, spending less . . .
Other people strive for fame;
I avoid the limelight, preferring to be left alone.
Indeed, I seem like an idiot:
no mind, no worries.
— 20

We have been taught that if we can just amass enough money, prestige, possessions, and protective gear, we will be safe and secure. Lao Tse assures us that well-being is not attained by manipulating the outer world. It is attained by stepping into our right mind. Happiness is not the result of conditions; it is born of attitude.

The Great Way does not demand that we stop shopping or give all of our stuff away. We can play with the things of the world. The Tao simply calls us to differentiate between *illusory wants* and *real needs*. All of your needs have been supplied by God and always will be. If you really need something in the material world, it will come without struggle or strain. When Dee and I discovered our new home on the market, we contacted the seller's agent and told him we were very interested. He informed us that the seller was in negotiation on a previously submitted offer. Although we were excited about the house, we decided to just place the deal in the hands of the Tao. If the house was to be ours, it would come to us. If not, the Tao would provide equal or better. A week later the agent informed us that the deal under consideration had fallen through. We submitted an offer, the seller accepted, and the house came to us as if orchestrated as part of a greater plan.

This brings us to a crucial point about how the Tao works. If a partner, job, or home belongs to you, it will be yours. If not, it will not come, and, believe me, you don't want it. Something else that is truly yours will find you. We own things not by money or paperwork, but by *right of consciousness*. What is yours will know your face. Trust me on this. When you recognize the riches you already own on the inside, all the riches you need will show up on the outside.

Those who know they have enough are rich.

—— 33

Who is wealthy?
He who is content with what he has.
— The Talmud

You Can't Outgive the Tao

If you wish to enjoy greater abundance, begin by understanding the universal principle of circulation. Money, like the blood in your body and the rain that makes living things grow, functions only when it is circulated. If you do not spend money and it just sits under your mattress, it loses value over time. The purpose of money is to pass it around. Then it prospers others, stimulates the economy, and returns to you multiplied.

If you are fearful about money or other possessions, you might hoard or hide them. Such stockpiling runs contrary to the Tao. The system of Chinese medicine is based on the flow of *chi*, life force. As long as chi is flowing, you are healthy. When chi is blocked or for any reason does not reach a part of the body, illness ensues. To restore health, get chi moving again.

Likewise, to be wealthy you must make active use of your money, which you can do in many different ways: purchase something; hire someone; invest in something; or give to charity. If you don't have a lot of money, don't use your bank balance as an excuse to not share whatever wealth you have. The anxious mind says, "I will give more when I have more," but the reverse is true: When you give more, you will have more. When you give, you affirm that you trust the universe will support you as you support others. I once offered a training for which I had one space open, and two people applied for it. One was a wealthy person who tried to bargain for a discount. The other was a person with not much money who offered all she could afford, a small portion of the tuition. I accepted the latter because her offer was a stretch for her and a sincere declaration of intention. It's not how much money you have or give that's important; it's the state of mind you live in.

If you do not have a lot of money to move, you can move your chi in other ways. You can volunteer at a service organization or create through art, music, writing, dance, theater, or building. You can teach, parent, pray for others, be intimate with your beloved, travel, or work toward political change. My friend George thrived on giving love. As an elder in an intentional community, he spent his latter days going from person to person, telling them how wonderful they were and how grateful he was for the gifts they brought to his life. All he did was spread love around. People in the community made fun of him, but this man had discovered the key to the riches that most people seek but do not find because they are looking in places that fail them. You can spend lots of money and still be painfully self-absorbed and feel poor. You can spend little money, but spread joy around, and you will walk in heaven even while you live on earth.

When you withhold money, kindness, or support from others, you are withholding wealth from yourself. It is a fundamental psychological principle that we expect others (and life) to do to us what we do to or for them. Generous people expect the universe to be generous with them, and it is. Stingy people expect the universe to withhold from them, and it does. Not because the universe is withholding—life is generous by nature—but because the act of withholding sets up a psychic barrier that prevents the withholder from recognizing the gifts laid at her door. When Jesus said, "Do unto others as you would have them to do unto you," he was actually saying, "What you do unto others you *are* doing unto yourself."

Do not wait for acts of love, generosity, or kindness to be returned to you. If you sit around expecting favors to come back, you miss the point of giving. The act of giving blesses you with the experience of prosperity at the moment you give. What comes later, or does not come, is not worth thinking or worrying about. There are greater gifts to be counted.

The wise never try to hold on to things.
The more you do for others, the more you have.
The more you give to others, the greater
your abundance.

—81

Simple Does It

I was standing in the aisle of a hardware store next to a fellow asking a salesman about how to fix a faucet. After a long discussion about repair methods and options, the customer said, "Nothing in life is simple, is it?" Hearing that, another customer standing a few feet away chimed in, "Sure it is, if you make it simple."

I laughed as I realized that I didn't need to climb the Himalayas to a remote ashram or take a university course in philosophy to learn how to live. The hardware store served the purpose on that day.

Life is simple unless we make it complicated. The ego thrives in complexity while the spirit thrives in simplicity. Where we live in the country we sometimes find centipedes in small, dark, enclosed spaces. If we leave any wooden boards behind the garage, when we pick them up we discover centipedes hiding under them. The moment these creatures are exposed to the light, they scamper away to find another dark place. The centipedes in our lives, the problems that sting us, hide in the convolutions and complexities we create or allow. The more complexity, the more issues. The more simplicity, the fewer difficulties. If you find yourself in a complicated situation, look for the simple way out. The scientific theorem Occam's razor, put forth by 14th-century English logician William of Occam, states, "The simplest answer tends to be the correct one." We have been led to believe that an answer is not valid unless it is complicated. But then again, we have been led to believe lots of things that are not true.

> *Primal Virtue goes deep and far.*
> *It leads all things back*
> *Toward the great oneness.*
>
> —— 65

Enough Is Enough

You are an abundant being living in an abundant universe that is ready, willing, and able to provide for all of your needs. Everyone in the world can be wealthy if we recognize the blessings seeded in and around us. *Tao Te Ching* is the simplest teaching to undo poverty thinking and restore us to the prosperity we deserve. Real wealth does not depend on worldly status or a bank balance. It is available in the sweeping cloud formations above you, the soft grass under your bare feet, the light in your children's eyes, and your funny cat. If we could realize the depth and extent of the gifts we have already been given, we would attain heights of ecstasy that collecting stuff will never achieve. Let us take refuge in the Tao as the never-ending source of our good.

As the soldiers approached Lao Tse's cabin, my heart clutched. Their stately horses bore the mantle of the royal guard, representing the emperor himself. The soldiers wore their brightest finery, jackets crimson as a summer sunset, swords gleaming in the light. Seeing this imposing entourage, my first impulse was to flee and take cover. But when Lao Tse emerged from his cabin and walked slowly toward them, his quiet demeanor comforted me.

"Are you Lao Tse?" the commanding officer called in a strong voice.

The master bowed his head. "At your service."

The leader dismounted, approached the elder sage, and offered a respectful bow.

"I have been dispatched by General Dou Xian, commander of the forces of Han. He needs guidance in the ongoing brutal war against Qin. Your reputation as a brilliant adviser has spread far and wide. General Xian wishes to offer you the honorable position of chief counselor. In exchange he will give you a mansion in a fine section of the city, a handsome salary, servants at your whim, and he will provide for all of your needs."

Lao Tse simply laughed and left a silence hanging. "I am the richest man in the world," he finally stated. "All my needs are already provided for. Why would I want to move to a mansion in a polluted city with people bickering at every turn and fearful throngs rushing about to nowhere?"

The commander's forehead wrinkled and his thick eyebrows raised almost to touch above his nose. He looked over the master's shoulder and scanned the crooked cabin, held together by warped wood and topped with a thatched roof badly in need of replacement. Then his eyes fell upon the yard, where a donkey was shooing a pig from its space, ducks were quacking as they bathed in a large mud puddle, and two mixed-breed dogs were lying belly up in the sun.

"With all respect, sir, this does not look like the home of a rich man."

"Then please look again, commander. A different kind of vision will show you a different kind of estate." The master turned and extended his arm to sweep the scene. "I awake each morning to the golden sun rising over those mountain peaks. As I enjoy my morning tea, I watch the mist rise from the valley like the whisper of a parting lover. Then I stroll through the bamboo forest amidst the song of legions of lavishly colored birds. At night the full moon bathes my bedroom walls with such a shimmering otherworldly glow that I must stay up far into the night to watch it." Lao Tse turned and pointed to the other side of the yard. "That pomegranate tree showers me with an endless bounty of delicious fruit, without me having to prove myself to earn its gift. These animals are my best friends. My dogs are more loyal to me than any human being has ever been. That donkey has never lied to me. The pig makes funny gurgling sounds when I scratch it behind the ears. I live in a state of grace. Why would I trade this heaven to live in a stuffy building in a stifling city, surrounded by a staff of gossiping servants, and go to work each day for a government obsessed with war?"

The commander again surveyed the house, mountains, bamboo forest, and the motley montage of critters. His face softened and a slight smile spread over his lips, as if he understood the master's teaching. For a moment, peace befell him. Then he reclaimed his military demeanor.

"So you are refusing General Dou's invitation?"

"No, I am fulfilling it. He wants direction in his war efforts. I shall give that free of charge. Tell him to inscribe these words on his sword: 'When planning revenge, be sure to dig two graves.' That is all he will need to know to guide his army."

The commander took a long breath as he realized he would get no further with this strange pundit. He bowed his head and extended his arms at chest height, his hands clasped together, the sign of humility. He mounted his horse and ordered his squadron to depart. Within minutes they were out of sight, leaving only the dust the horses kicked up at their exit.

Lao Tse put his arm around my shoulder and guided me back to the cabin. "Come, let us enjoy my palace," he laughed. "One day I will fix the roof—or maybe not." The dogs rose and followed us into the tiny abode. Lao Tse patted them both on the head, the ducks followed, and the donkey brayed. The master picked up a duck, held it against his chest, smoothed its neck with his hand, and kissed it on its head.

Truly I have never seen a richer man.

Therefore those who know that enough is
enough will always have enough.

—— 46

A REASON,
A SEASON,
A LIFETIME

In action, watch the timing.

— 8

The master and I arose early one morning and walked into the village to purchase groceries from the market. As we stood above an old round-faced woman seated on the ground selling oranges from a blanket spread before her, I noticed Lao Tse's eyes drawn to a young woman purchasing chestnuts at a stand ten paces away. The master seemed lost in his gaze at her. She was radiant, long shiny black hair drifting over one shoulder, tied by a clip of colored beads. Her dark eyes were set off by high regal cheekbones. When she smiled at the merchant, her face cast a beam all the way to where we were standing.

"Are you attracted to that woman?" I asked Lao Tse. As soon as those words left my mouth, I felt embarrassed. Never before had I probed into the master's love life. He lived a reclusive, hermit-like existence, and I assumed his interest in the fair gender had either waned or been supplanted by his spiritual walk.

"She reminds me of my wife," he answered.

I was stunned. "You have a wife?"

"I had a wife. She died in childbirth."

I didn't know what to say. This was all a great revelation. "I'm sorry," I offered awkwardly.

He turned and faced me. "I cherished her for the time we were together. I grieved when she died. I am mostly over it, but sometimes I still miss her."

Lao Tse bowed to the merchant and walked on toward the stall where the dazzling woman had been standing. By now she had moved on.

"Would you consider marrying again?"

He shrugged. "If something like that happens, it happens. If not, I am content with myself."

He continued through the market with me pacing him at his side.

"Marriage is usually not an expression of the Tao," he went on. "More often it springs from insecurity and fear. People are pushed into marriage by their parents, religion, or culture. Or they wish to gain financial security, raise their social status, or be envied for their 'catch.' It's all political, and has nothing to do with the choice of the heart. Politics and the Tao rarely find themselves in the same bed."

Never before had we discussed marriage. I felt shaky in unexplored territory. "What about people who marry for love? Are they flowing with the Tao?"

The master turned and placed his hand on my shoulder to underscore his message. "If they truly love, yes. But many people confuse love with physical impulses, fantasy, or escape from loneliness. Then when they get with their partner they feel even lonelier. You cannot fill a false emptiness. Those who know they are already full do not need someone to make them whole."

"So you don't believe in marriage?"

"I believe in the Great Way," he answered firmly. "If the Tao draws two people together, and they are happy, the union is made in heaven. A parchment with the seal of a priest or government official does not make people married. Either they are joined in spirit, or they are not. If they are joined, there is happiness. If not, there is sorrow."

We went on with our shopping and dropped the subject. I never asked him about his wife again. He never volunteered any more information. This was the one pain I saw him carry.

Let It Be What It Wants to Be

Every relationship has a purpose. There is no such thing as an accidental, random, or mistaken relationship. Everyone we attract serves our soul's growth. Sometimes that growth comes through joy, and sometimes through challenge. When we receive the gift the relationship came to deliver, its purpose is fulfilled. In some cases that fulfillment moves us to continue the relationship and deepen it, and in other cases it moves us to part. This is the way of the Tao.

Relationships come to us for a *reason*, a *season*, or a *lifetime*. *Reason* relationships might occur via a brief meeting where paths cross for a meaningful moment. When I stepped into the elevator of a hotel in Hawaii, for example, I shared the short ride with a couple. "How is your vacation going?" I asked.

"Okay, I guess," the wife replied, looking less than gleeful.

"Why not so great?"

"I have a kidney stone that is quite painful," she explained. "I'll either have to keep taking medication with unpleasant side effects, or have surgery when I get home."

I felt sad to see this woman resign herself to pain. "I'm sorry to hear that," I told her. "I know a number of people who have dealt successfully with kidney stones. There are some flushes you can do by ingesting certain herbs mixed with juices. You might want to google 'holistic remedies for kidney stones.' Maybe you can get this handled more easily."

"Really?" the woman lit up. "I will surely look that up. Thank you so much!"

The couple reached their floor, the elevator door opened, and they stepped out. I marveled at the import of our interaction. In 30 seconds we shared a connection that could potentially prove healing and get a human being out of pain.

When my friends Tom and Haley met, they knew they were soul mates, and began to spend all their time together. Three months later Haley was pregnant, and soon afterward the couple had a small wedding ceremony. In the fullness of time a beautiful boy, Jason, arrived in the world and became the light of their life.

After a few years, tensions between Tom and Haley arose and their marriage started to crumble. Haley fell for another guy and left Tom. Although their divorce was rocky, both parents remained committed to their son.

Over the years Jason grew into a fine young man and his parents were proud of him. The couple reinvented their relationship as friends and joined together to support their son. Eventually Haley remarried and she invited Tom to the wedding. While sitting in the church waiting for Haley to walk down the aisle, another guest asked Tom, "How do you know the bride?" Tom answered nonchalantly, "I used to be married to her."

Tom and Haley's marriage lasted but a short time, but their relationship with their son continues for their lifetime. We might say that (besides the relationship lessons they both learned) the purpose of their union was to bring forth their son. Once that happened, they did not have a lot to do with each other. Their belief that they were soul mates was the glue that got them together. Tom and Haley were more learning mates than soul mates. But they were both truly soul mates with their son.

Other relationships exist for a *season*. You may be married to someone for a number of years, or work at a company, or share a dear friendship, or study with a spiritual mentor for a period of time. Then the season comes to an end. Such a moment can be confusing because we tend to think in terms of "always" when we enter into an intimate or important relationship. We like the security of feeling that this person will always be who they are to us. But nothing in form, Lao Tse assures us, is for always. Everything changes. One day everything you can touch with your fingers will not be here. Your body will not be here. Your house will not be here. The city you live in and your country will not be here. One day the planet Earth will not be here, or the sun around which it revolves. Nothing in form stays forever. Resist change and you suffer. Accept it and you are free.

In contrast to things that come and go, the Tao is eternal. Its reality transcends the temporal. The Tao will remain after all things return to it. Trusting in the Tao yields a security that nothing in the world delivers. Participate in the world, but establish yourself in that which goes far beyond it.

The ten thousand things rise and fall while the self watches their return.

They grow and flourish and then return to the source.

Returning to the source is stillness, which is the way of nature.

— 16

Take refuge in the constant. If you seek security in anything that passes, you will be sad upon its departure. This does not mean we are to distance ourselves from relationships, deny ourselves the joy they bring, or rebuff sorrow when they depart. To the contrary, knowing that one day those close to you will not be here enriches relationships while you have them. When you are with people you love, imagine you may never see them again. Be fully present with them. Speak the words you wish for them to hear. Thank, honor, acknowledge, and celebrate them. They are in your life for a blessed season that bestows its unique gifts. Don't miss a moment of loving. Leave nothing unsaid or undone. Then, when it is time for you or the other person to disappear back into the Tao, your soul will say, "Well done."

Lifetime relationships run the deepest and offer us the most soul growth. Their value is inestimable. Such relationships may include your parents, siblings, spouse, children, and other significant family members. You may also have certain dear friends, business associates, or spiritual colleagues for life. You have entered into a sacred soul contract. Discover what it is and bless it.

Soul mates are not just romantic partners; they are all the people with whom you connect at a soul level. Some soul mates bring you immense delight, and others are extremely challenging. Some are both. If you have a long-term difficult relationship with someone, ask the Tao to reveal to you the lesson that relationship is offering you. As I mentioned, problems exist only until you extract the gifts they bring. This is especially true in difficult relationships. Once you discover the gift and unwrap it, the problem has served its purpose and it evaporates. Then you may connect more deeply or go separate ways with a sense of completion.

The secret to successful relationships is to let every relationship be what it wants to be. We experience confusion, conflict, and disappointment in relationships when we try to make them into something other than what they are. You may struggle to turn a brief connection into a long-term relationship, or stretch a season relationship into a lifetime. Ask each relationship to reveal its purpose to you. Accept the blessing offered rather than the one you are trying to fabricate, and your relationships will flow seamlessly.

You might also take a season or lifetime relationship and attempt to shorten or get rid of it. Neither will you succeed at this. If you try to end a relationship before it has fulfilled its purpose, it will just keep coming back. Many couples break up or get divorced, and other individuals distance themselves from families or friends. But somehow life draws them together again—always for good reasons. (I know one couple who divorced and remarried three times.) You cannot escape a relationship that has a destiny to fulfill. Running away won't work; you must graduate. Until then, the Tao will bond you and the other person with cosmic superglue.

When a relationship has served its purpose, there is no use to try to hang onto it. A Chinese adage advises, "When your horse dies, get off." I have coached countless people who tell me, "I had a good friend for a long time. But I have changed and I no longer find reward in being with her. She is quite negative, complains, and wants to engage in gossip and shallow talk. I used to join her in such conversations, but now I feel bored and irritated. I don't want to accept her invitations, but I feel guilty to say no because we have always been good friends." I tell such clients, "What was, was. What is, is. Be true to what is, rather than clinging to an old form. Then you will create new meaningful relationships that match who you are and what you want."

A Course in Miracles tells us that it is the destiny of all relationships to resolve into peace. No matter how negative or painful a relationship is, one day it will be healed. Perhaps you will enjoy this transformation in this lifetime or perhaps another. Or perhaps the relationship will be healed at a soul level and you will not see the manifestation in the material world. Many years ago a friend got upset with me and he stopped speaking to me. Yet over the years I have had many dreams of us connecting. In the dreams we are always having a good time and loving each other. At a soul level, there has been no lapse in our deep friendship. Only in the world of appearances, which are always illusory, have we been apart.

If you are separated from someone, or they turn their back on you, or someone has passed on, don't despair. You can connect with them in spirit. In prayer or meditation call this person to you. See his or her face before you. Then speak to that person's soul. Imagine he or she could hear you and receive your message. What would you like to say to this person if you knew your communication would sink in? What would that person like you to know? Cultivate your relationship in spirit, and two things will happen: (1) Your soul will come to peace; and (2) You will maximize your power to manifest a better relationship with that person on the physical plane. Because we are spiritual beings at our core, it is the *spirit* of a relationship that brings us fulfillment. It matters less what the bodies are doing. You may live under the same roof with someone and sleep beside them, yet feel worlds apart. You may also have friends at a far distance with whom you feel deeply united. Relationships are about souls more than bodies.

The Tao is always working to bring you relationships that feed your soul, and to move you away from relationships that tatter your soul. Just as the earth has cycles and seasons, so do your connections with others. Do not settle for shallow or empty interactions. Ask that each relationship becomes what it wants to be, and that you become your full self in all of your interactions. The Tao is striving to bring you the happiness you seek, and it needs your cooperation. Don't try to impose your will over what wants to be. Ultimately your will *is* what wants to be. Let life join you with those who belong to you, and release everyone and everything else to find its right place in the vast domain of the Great Way.

To be interested in the changing seasons
is a happier state of mind than
to be hopelessly in love with spring.
— GEORGE SANTAYANA

THIS YEAR'S NEST

*Look always forward. In last year's nests . . .
there are no birds this year.*

— From *Don Quixote* by Miguel de Cervantes

If there is one thing in the world that we can depend on, it is change. Lao Tse calls us to not resist change, but to let it empower us. The more you fight change, the more it overwhelms you. The more you flow with it, the more it strengthens you. The river of life takes many twists and turns. The sage does not attempt to paddle back upstream, but delights in the mystery of where the new twists and turns lead.

*If you realize that all things change,
there is nothing you will try to hold on to.
If you are not afraid of dying,
there is nothing you cannot achieve.*

—— 74

Yoga master Paramahansa Yogananda advised, "What comes of itself, let it come. What goes of itself, let it go." Yet many of us fight to hold on to what wants to leave, and we keep at a distance what wants to come in its stead. A seminar participant told me, "I leave claw marks on everything I have to let go of." The human psyche is a strange creation. We believe that the known is always preferable to the unknown, even if the known sucks. Eighty percent of women in abusive relationships either stay in them or leave and enter another abusive situation. The twisted reasoning behind this pattern is, "My world is painful but at least it is predictable. I can navigate the familiar, but I may not be able to control the unfamiliar. I can tolerate my current despicable situation, but I may not survive in uncharted territory. The devil I know is better than the devil I do not know."

But what if the devil you know could be replaced by an angel? What if life is always moving us to greater good? What if your past or your current situation has played itself out, and something greater awaits? What if you are being called to fulfill a higher destiny?

A Course in Miracles tells us that it takes great maturity to recognize that *all* events, encounters, relationships, and changes are helpful. Trust is the bedrock of a spiritual master's entire belief system. "Trust would settle every problem now," the Course states plainly.

Trust in the Tao empowers us to move ahead in the face of adversity and uncertainty. Faith is the invisible safety net that helps 20 percent of women break out of abusive situations and create more self-honoring relationships. It is the unflinching ally of those who overcome addictions and conquer self-demeaning habits. It is the torch of hope for those who leave bad marriages, jobs, or living situations and trust that life will take them to a better place. Such people recognize that behind the appearances of change, grace is present. Your faith may not yet be perfect as you step ahead; doubts and fears may still assail you. But even a small step is enough to begin the journey home.

*A tree as great as a man's embrace springs
from a small shoot;*
A terrace nine stories high begins with a pile of earth;
A journey of a thousand miles starts under one's feet.

—— 64

Golden Intersections

If we fear to take that first step ahead, we might be tempted to glamorize the past or reactivate it to escape present discontent. Lao Tse would urge us to avoid efforts to drag the past into the present. If the past wants to be activated, it will do so. Otherwise, you are better off to just let it be what it was, and trust that what is here now is so for a reason.

I used to regret that I missed out on opportunities in past relationships. I would romanticize them in my mind, thinking, "I should have stayed with her," or "If I had been a better partner, maybe we would still be together." Yet *in every case* some uncanny experience or messenger appeared to show me there was a reason those relationships did not endure. For example, my first amour was my girlfriend Laurie, whom I met in my college class in New Jersey. I was high on love for that entire semester until Laurie transferred to another school. Then we had a stormy breakup and I never saw Laurie again. Over the years I wondered if we might have continued our romance and come together for life if I had handled the situation better.

Thirty-five years later, a friend of mine invited me to a small dinner party at his home in a remote mountain town in Maui. "I want you to meet my friend Eddie from Oregon," he told me. When I arrived I was shocked to discover that this Eddie was Laurie's brother! Eventually our conversation came around to Laurie, and I admitted I felt bad about our breakup. "No need," Eddie told me. "The lifestyle Laurie has chosen is worlds away from what you are doing. I assure you that you have nothing in common these days." Then he told me about

Laurie's volatile relationships and gnarly breakups. Still I gave him my e-mail address to pass along to his sister so I could at least say hello after all these years. Laurie never responded. The Tao was helping me finally cut the cord. Now I realize that ending the relationship, even for what seemed foolish or immature reasons, was for the best. It is said, "Man's [or woman's] rejection is God's protection."

Another way I have attempted to activate the past is by feeling indebted to people who have helped me. One minister, for example, supported me in important ways to launch my career. When I saw him years later, he had quit ministry and gone into the auto business. We no longer had much to talk about. Another friend had generously loaned me a sum of money when I needed help. Although I had paid her back promptly, I still felt ingratiated to her. When I saw her years later, she had gotten involved in a multilevel marketing enterprise and she began to hound me to become a downline. She was not the same person I once knew and our relationship was not what it once was. While I forever appreciate these good people for their help and I honor the new paths they have chosen, I realized that our journeys no longer intertwined as they once did. Through these and similar experiences I recognize that (1) these people were not the *source* of my good, but in those moments of kindness they were acting as loving vehicles through which the true Source, the Tao, was delivering my good; (2) the moments during which we met were a kind of "golden intersection" when the time was right for us to mutually benefit; and (3) I need to accept that life has moved us on to new and different places, perfect for each of us.

When we understand how golden intersections work, we can step forward with gratitude and confidence, accepting what is rather than fantasizing about what was or what could be. The film *The Curious Case of Benjamin Button* presents the fantasy tale of a man who is born old and grows younger. Meanwhile the woman who is the love of his life is moving from youth to old age. The time comes when the two meet and enjoy a passionate and soulful connection. But because he is growing younger and she is growing older, at some point they no longer match and they must each go on with their unique journeys.

Likewise, in many relationships there is a period of ripeness during which we connect and uplift each other's lives. When that phase is complete, it is time to move on. Attempting to hold on will only create frustration and delay the next golden intersection. As much as we would like to hold on to sweet situations forever, we must let go when they have run their course. This is the way of the Tao.

Lest you grow wistful because golden intersections do not last forever, take comfort in knowing that (1) you can still love and appreciate the person and the time you shared even if you are no longer together; (2) there is always another (often better) golden intersection coming to replace the one that ended; and (3) some golden relationships *do* last a lifetime and perhaps many lifetimes. The Great Way, Lao Tse would assure us, is never devoid of gold.

In my hometown I had been studying with two famous martial arts masters who had joined to create an academy. When they taught together, the energy was mythic. Their synergy seemed to call the very gods from heaven. Those classes gained renown and were filled to overflowing. I never missed a session.

Then the two teachers had a falling-out. They accused each other of various indiscretions and they parted ways. Controversy and gossip followed in the wake, and students were urged to follow one or the other. The drama of their parting was quite distressing for me. I could not understand why two gifted teachers could split apart when their chemistry together was so magnificent. It seemed that they had fallen from their lofty perches to the dregs of human personality. Bitter and confused, I could not bring myself to choose one or the other. For that matter, I did not wish to see either. I went to Lao Tse and told him of my upset.

"You just failed martial arts," he told me.

His remark disarmed me. "How did I do that? I have been studying with these teachers for years and I am approaching an advanced belt."

"The secret of martial arts is to take the power your opponent directs against you, and use it for your benefit."

Yes, I had learned that. But what did it have to do with my current dilemma?

"In this case your opponent is not a person. It is the force of change. Your resistance to the teachers' parting is weakening you. If you accept it as a fact of life, you will regain your power."

As I tried to absorb the master's insight, he walked to a cabinet and took out a sword. He had shown me the weapon once before; it was a gift from a warrior who had renounced battle so he could become Lao Tse's student.

He handed the gleaming weapon to me. As the cold steel touched my hands I felt powerful just holding it.

"Now give me the sword," the master ordered.

I followed his instruction. Suddenly he took a swipe at my head. I ducked and spouted a nervous laugh. I looked at him incredulously.

"You just gave me your power. Now you are at my mercy." He took another swipe, this time closer. I backed away. Would this go on all day?

"Now, take back your power." The master extended the sword toward me, clutching it with both hands. I hesitated to reach for it, not wanting to engage in combat with my mentor.

"Go ahead, do as I say."

I took a breath and tried to grab the sword from him. He resisted. I tried harder, until we were wrestling for the weapon. Finally I pulled it from his grasp. I'm sure he could have held on to it, but he wanted me to learn the lesson. We straightened up and dusted ourselves off.

"Now you have your power back," said Lao Tse. "Don't give it away to me or anyone, ever again."

The lesson was starting to sink in. "The sword represents the power I gave to my teachers?"

"You gave your power to the condition of them teaching together. If they are together, you are happy. If they are not together, you are unhappy. This is not the way of the Tao. It is the way of the fool. You cannot afford to allow your happiness to depend on any external situation. You must find the source of your happiness within you. Then nothing in the outside world will be able to remove your peace."

I handed the weapon back to the master and he replaced it in the cabinet. Silently he left the room, leaving me to ponder how I had given my power away in many areas of my life.

Therefore the wise are guided by what they feel
and not by what they see,

Letting go of that and choosing this.

— 12

Time and Timing

In the book of Ecclesiastes we are told, "To everything there is a season, and a time to every purpose under heaven." This maxim captures the essence of the Great Way. The Tao imbues people and events with life force for a purpose and a time. When that purpose is fulfilled, the life force is withdrawn. To try to bring life force to something from which it has been withdrawn is futile. To try to remove life force from where it is flowing is also futile. The secret of mastery is to find where life force is flowing and move with it.

Human beings are unique in creation for our ability to be somewhere other than here, by mentally and emotionally drifting into the past and future. Genius inventor Buckminster Fuller said, "Human beings are the only creatures on the planet that tell time and think they have to earn a living." The present moment is fully embodied; the past and future are ghosts. Reality exists only now.

Regret is time doubly wasted. If you made a mistake, you may believe that a moment or years were for naught. If you regret your mistake, you are wasting the current moment as well. If you learned from the mistake, the time and experience were worthwhile.

A coaching client who had gotten a divorce complained, "I wasted 20 years of my life."

I asked her, "Did you enjoy the years you loved your husband and the marriage worked?"

"Yes, I did."

"And did you learn from the process of choosing to get divorced?"

"Absolutely."

"And are you a better and stronger person for having gone through the whole experience?"

"For sure."

"Then none of that time was wasted," I explained. "All of it, including the good times and the hard times, have brought you to the powerful place where you now stand."

The Great Way calls us to extract the blessings and lessons and move on. Rather than going over what happened, maximize what can happen now. Master the task at hand, and the past will be replaced by the treasures the current moment offers. When I interviewed Dominic Miller, the guitarist in Sting's band, I asked him what he had learned in such an auspicious position. "For one thing, you can't dwell on your mistakes," he answered. "If you're playing a concert and you miss a note, you can't say, 'Hey, everybody, I just messed up. Let's stop and play that section again.' You have to just let it be and move where the music is going instead of getting stuck where it was."

Wishing and waiting for something better to happen is also a misuse of the current moment. The ego manufactures seeming gaps between where you are and what you want. When Buddha taught that desire is the cause of suffering, he meant that when you crave something you do not have and you believe you cannot be happy until you get it, you are missing the immense fulfillment available to you here and now. Like Buddha, Lao Tse would have us milk every moment of life.

The Tao is an empty vessel; it is used, but never filled.

— 4

This Too Shall Pass

We all have days or phases where adversity seems to pile up against us. We wonder if the universe is conspiring to see how many things could go wrong at once. How, then, do you navigate a stretch when you feel totally overwhelmed or your life seems to be falling apart?

1. **Surrender.** Quit fighting what's happening and let events play themselves out. You are kayaking on a rapidly moving river. Just go with it. Know that this phase is temporary and you will emerge into calmer waters.

   High winds do not last all morning.

   Heavy rain does not last all day.

   Why is this? Heaven and earth!

   If heaven and earth cannot make things last forever,

   How is it possible for us?

   — 23

2. **Trust** that you are never given any challenge beyond your ability to handle and master.

3. **Find the good**, the blessing, and the healing. How are these changes serving you in ways you would not have experienced had they not come about? What fixed position are these upheavals dislodging you from, opening you to broader dimensions of life? How are you being redirected in helpful ways?

4. **Nurture yourself** by doing things that renew your spirit. Any activity that puts you in a positive state of mind will help you see clearly and make healthy choices that lead to resolution.

5. **Ask for help** from people, your angels, Higher Power, the Tao, or any other Source you trust and believe in. Reach out. Pray. Don't be stubborn, attempt to do it all yourself, or be righteously sacrificial. The Tao will make your course easier, through people who love you and synchronistic events, if you let it.

Nothing in the world is permanent, including hard times. Hang in there, be kind to yourself, stay connected to your spiritual source, and you will emerge with unexpected gifts. That's a promise.

> *So sometimes things are ahead and*
> *sometimes they are behind;*
> *Sometimes breathing is hard, sometimes it comes easily;*
> *Sometimes there is strength, and sometimes weakness;*
> *Sometimes one is up and sometimes down.*
>
> — *29*

Onward!

Creative people are more concerned with what is enlivening now rather than what was stimulating last month or year. After I launch a book, I think little about it. The next book is far more exciting. If you are an artist, writer, designer, musician, actor, entrepreneur, teacher, or leader, you understand this dynamic. Last year's book was the product of last year's thoughts. Those thoughts remain valid and important; the people who can benefit from them will find them and use them. Meanwhile, I am far more interested in the new thoughts that stand on the shoulders of the old ones. My marketing staff wants me to keep plugging recent books, and I cooperate where I can. But to me creating is more meaningful than selling. The magic, I have discovered, is that if I imbue my passion in a product, it sells. There are other people whose joy and talent are anchored in marketing. So I let them exercise their skill and delight while I exercise mine. Somehow it all fits. The Tao is a cosmic jigsaw puzzle in which all the pieces join together perfectly. Each of us simply has to be true to the shape of our piece and not try to stuff ourselves into a shape that doesn't match us.

Here is a sample dialogue of how I coach clients who are trying to find their career direction or life path:

"What would be the most exciting thing you would like to do next?"

"Well, I was trained in accounting."

"Even though you have had that training, what would you like to do at this time?"

"I managed a store once."

"Good. But that was then. What is now?"

"My parents always wanted me to have a secure job and now I have one. My husband is concerned about our income."

"Got it. If pressure from your parents and husband were not an issue, what would you like to do?"

"I don't know."

"If you did know, what would you know?"

"I can't think of anything that I could earn an income at besides accounting."

"Don't try to figure it out. Use your imagination. Be creative. What would you love to do if money and experience were no object?"

"I really enjoy outdoor photography."

"Now we are on to something! If you were to photograph outdoors, where would you do it?"

"There's a state park about an hour from my house. I could go there on weekends and shoot."

"Fabulous! Is there any way you might earn an income from photography?"

"Well, my cousin works for a stock photography company. They have a catalog of outdoor shots. Not to brag, but I think I could do better."

"It's not bragging to be honest about where your passion and talent live. Now you need to follow it."

"Do you really think I could succeed at photography?"

"I think that what you are most passionate about is the strongest magnet to bring you reward on many levels."

When we release what was, then what is or what could be has space to be born. Children are the happiest people on the planet because they are not dragging the baggage of a long heavy past around with them. If they trip and fall or get upset, they get over it quickly. Nor are they pondering or planning what comes next. The now moment provides them with all the entertainment and fulfillment they need. At some point we all got hung up on time and we abandoned the current moment. We have distracted ourselves with what is not here. Yet the now moment is always available for us to reclaim our soul. At any instant we can step back into heaven. Lao Tse would urge us to pitch our tent right here, the only place life truly lives.

> *Open your eyes! The world is still intact;*
> *it is as pristine as it was on the first day,*
> *as fresh as milk!*
>
> — Paul Claudel

LOVE HOW MUCH
YOU HATE IT

The devils in our life are angels who
prod us to move on to where we would rather be.

When I arrived at the master's cottage, I did not want him to see me so upset; surely he would realize I had lost the Tao. But the moment I greeted him, I knew my façade had failed. "What's the matter?" he asked.

I shook my head, trying to put him off.

He reached for his walking stick and said, "Let's take a walk."

Lao Tse, old now yet still spry, linked his arm under my elbow and guided me through his herb garden to the edge of the bamboo forest that bordered his little parcel of land. Immediately the hypnotic sound of the bamboo stalks clicking against each other in the wind began to relax me. We stepped into this mystical kingdom and strolled silently along the path softly carpeted by fallen leaves.

"Now, what is it?" he asked.

I took a breath and began to vent. "A few days ago I went down to the dock to see if I could get some work to earn money to make my journey to come and see you. There I found a leathery-skinned man supervising some younger guys hauling fish from a boat. I asked him if he had any work for me."

"'Are you strong?' he asked.

"'Certainly.'

"'Will you show up for work?'

THE TAO MADE EASY

"'I am very dependable.'

"'Very well, then. Start now and work for me for the next two days. I will pay you on the third morning.'"

Lao Tse nodded pensively, as if he knew where the story was headed.

"What did you feel about this man who hired you?" he asked, a shaft of sunlight glistening for a moment off his forehead.

"I had a bad feeling about him. He was gruff and had a dark look in his eyes, like my uncle who used to steal *baijiu* and sell it behind the tavern. I didn't like him and something inside told me this was not going to work out well."

"Then why didn't you listen to your instinct?"

"I was afraid that if I didn't get the job I would not have the money to come see you. I also wanted to trust the Tao. I figured that if the Tao had brought me to this man, there must be a reason."

By now we were well into the bamboo forest, bathed in deep shadow. The master ambled slowly at my side, listening attentively to my tale. "And then?"

"I worked hard for two days and returned the next morning for my wages. But the man and his boat were not there. I searched for him for a while, to no avail. Finally I asked a fisherman if he had seen my boss. 'He sailed away at sunrise with his crew,' he told me. 'He won't be back.' Hearing that, I grew furious! I had worked hard and trusted this man, and he cheated me. I remained upset for my entire journey here. Without money, I had to beg for food. Fortunately, people were kind and offered me rice and vegetables. One family took me in for lunch. I hoped to be rid of my anger by the time I arrived to see you, but I could not hide from your knowing eyes."

Just then we reached a small clearing. The master sat down on a large rock and motioned for me to join him.

"You were correct," said Lao Tse, leaning his hands on his stick. "The Tao did bring you together with that man for a reason. It's just not the one you thought it was."

I looked at him with consternation.

"When you had a bad feeling about working for that fisherman, that was the Tao giving you guidance. You chose to override that intuition because you were afraid about money. You also made an unwise assumption that just because you were brought to that man, you were supposed to work with him."

"But you have taught me that it is always important to trust."

"In this case it was more important for you to trust your inner guidance than to trust that man. People are not always trustworthy. The Tao will never let you down."

When the master spoke, everything seemed simple and clear, even obvious.

"What a fool I was!"

Lao Tse shook his head and laid his hand over mine. "Don't be too hard on yourself. This experience bestowed you with an important lesson."

I thought about what that might be. "To trust my inner voice and act on it?"

He smiled. "That, my friend, is the teaching of a lifetime. If you are now keener to follow the voice of the Tao when it prompts you, don't you think that a few days' work hauling fish is worth an insight that will last all your years and save you much struggle?"

For the first time since the incident, I began to feel relieved. Maybe it wasn't all bad.

"There was one more important lesson," he added, leaving a silence for me to tell what I thought it was. I searched my mind. I couldn't come up with anything.

"Even though you didn't earn the money for your journey here, you were provided for. Did you not eat well during your travels?"

"I did, thanks to the kindness of people in some villages along the way."

"That was the Tao caring for you through them. If the Tao does not supply your need through one avenue, it will deliver it through another pathway. You thought that your prosperity was to come through that job. But it came anyway, even without those wages. Can you see how brilliantly the Tao provides? And how this experience that seemed like a loss turned out to be a gain?"

I nodded. Lao Tse could make sense out of anything.

Sometimes we gain more from getting what we don't want than from getting what we do want. Mistakes may cost us in the mundane world, but when seen from a higher perspective they benefit us far more than the value of what we believe we have lost. In the Tao, there is no real loss.

If we allowed ourselves to face and feel the pain in our lives, it would serve its function to get our attention to recognize that we have stepped away from the Tao and we need to get back on course. It is said, "Love how much you hate it." If you are doing something you find repulsive, or you have had a bad experience, use your disgust as a motivator to change direction. When you are sick of it enough you will do something about it. *A Course in Miracles* tells us,

> *Tolerance for pain may be high, but it is not without limit.*
> *Eventually everyone begins to recognize, however dimly,*
> *that there must be a better way. As this recognition becomes*
> *more firmly established, it becomes a turning point.*

Lao Tse said it this way:

> *Knowing ignorance is strength.*
> *Ignoring knowledge is sickness.*
> *If one is sick of sickness, then one is not sick.*
> *The wise are not sick because they are sick of sickness.*
> *Therefore they are not sick.*
> —— 71

Be grateful, then, that you are sick and tired of being sick and tired, or fed up with what is not feeding you. Toleration of dysfunction only keeps it in force. Refuse to put up with what is not working, and you will find your way to your perfect place in the Great Design.

The story is told about a soldier who worked in an office on an army base. One day he began to pull papers out of a filing cabinet and study them. "That's not it!" he exclaimed after examining each one. He went on to repeat this process for hours.

The soldier's supervising officer watched this weird behavior and decided that the man was having a breakdown. So he sent him to the army psychologist. When the soldier entered the psychologist's office, he went to a file cabinet, picked out papers as he had in his original office, and continually exclaimed, "That's not it!"

After observing the soldier for 10 minutes, the psychologist concluded that the fellow had indeed lost his wits and he was no longer fit for duty. The shrink took out a pen and paper and wrote the soldier an order discharging him from the service.

The soldier took the paper, read it, and exclaimed, "That's it!"

We too, are continually noticing what is "It"—the Tao—and what is "Not It"—all that keeps us from what makes our heart sing. Unlike the soldier, however, many of us continue to accept situations that are clearly "Not It." We stay in jobs we hate; put up with stifling relationships; attend schools that fill our head with facts but leave our soul hungry; stress to fulfill boring social obligations; and subject ourselves to an endless stream of depressing news. If we were true to the voice of the Tao speaking to us through our instincts, we would be as honest as the soldier rejecting papers irrelevant to his intention. We would charge forward to find and celebrate the one paper we value—the Great Way. It takes courage to leave behind the world you have been taught is so important, and instead claim what is right for you. Ultimately we must, as Walt Whitman urged, "Dismiss whatever insults your soul."

> *Under heaven all can see beauty as beauty only*
> *because there is ugliness.*
> *All can know good as good only because there is evil.*
>
> —— *2*

Keep Hopping

You did not lose the Tao by falling off a cliff into a bottomless chasm one day. You slipped away from it in millions of small, steady steps. Psychologists have identified a phenomenon called "drift." Experimenters placed a group of frogs in a tub of water at room temperature, and the frogs thrived. Then the experimenters raised the temperature of the water gradually, ever so slightly, by a degree every few days. The frogs then adapted to the temperature as it increased. They became so adept at adjusting to the increasing temperature, in fact, that they stayed until the water became so hot that they died. When their gradual adaptation reached a fatal threshold, they had lost their ability to discern between what was life-sustaining and what was killing them. In some ways we as a species have not evolved much further than the frogs. We have become so accustomed to dysfunction and toxicity that we fail to recognize when it has passed a critical threshold. Yet there is a small but growing segment of the population that has retained its sensitivity to what is right, and is committed to thriving rather than just surviving. That would be you.

My client Ted's life had slipped into abysmal numbness. His marriage was in the pits, he hated his job, and he did not feel well. He was a real-life analog to Joe Banks in the humorous yet profound movie *Joe Versus the Volcano*. Ted figured he would just have to put up with his painful predicament because, well, that's just the way life is, and everybody does it. Then one day his 11-year-old daughter told him, "Dad, you're a ghost." *That* got his attention. Ted realized that the only person he had been fooling was himself. He was miserable and he had to do something about it. He quit his job, got a divorce, and set out on a brighter path. When I last saw Ted he was shining. The Tao spoke to Ted through his daughter, as it does through people who love us enough to be honest with us. I am not suggesting that you need to get a divorce or quit your job, although either could be an option. I *am* suggesting that you do whatever it takes to keep your soul alive. Sometimes that requires a change of circumstances, and sometimes it requires a shift of attitude.

In either case, you must assume the power and responsibility to claim your maximal happiness. When the pond gets too hot, it's time to jump.

Bless your wake-up calls. They are the Tao benevolently reaching from reality into illusion to rescue you from further pain. The world has drifted unspeakably far from its origin and intention, and is not a worthy guide to what is right, true, and healing. Daily we accept greed, charlatanry, thievery, warfare, pollution, starvation, and political doublespeak as if this is just the way we were born to live. *It is not.* In many ways the world we have fabricated is the precise inverse of the Tao. Every now and then an expansive thinker comes along and yells, "People, wake up! This can't be it! There is so much more available to you!" A few listeners heed the call and step onto the Great Way. But most people prefer to stay asleep. Illusion is enticing and self-reinforcing. Yet no matter how thick, dark, or painful the illusion becomes, the door to redemption is open. When we are ready to admit that the dream we were sold has become a nightmare, we will wake up to the Tao and find it welcoming us with open arms.

All healthy change begins with honesty. Tell the truth about what is "It" for you and what is "Not It." Be grateful for the "Not Its" as crucial redirectors toward "It." Take the smallest step into a new room, and you will gain entrée to vast worlds you could not see when you clung to the familiar. Acknowledge who you are and how you want to live, and the doors to your destiny will swing open before you.

Know the white,

But keep the black!

Be an example to the world!

Being an example to the world,

Ever true and unwavering,

Return to the infinite.

—— 28

THE PILLARS
OF VIRTUE

Cultivate Virtue in yourself,
And Virtue will be real.
Cultivate it in the family,
And Virtue will abound.
Cultivate it in the village,
And Virtue will grow.
Cultivate it in the nation,
And Virtue will be abundant.
Cultivate it in the universe,
And Virtue will be everywhere.

—— 54

Sitting on the bullet train hurtling from Osaka to Tokyo, my Japanese sponsor explained to me how that country has risen from the ashes since World War II. During the war, Japan was leveled by American bombing. The Japanese had to rebuild almost their entire nation. "Do you know what enabled Japan to be resurrected?" she asked me.

"Please tell me."

"The shared value of virtue. Those who survived the war were committed to harmony, cooperation, integrity, and achievement."

In our culture, *virtue* is not a word we use or hear very often. It rings of religious righteousness or Arthurian myth. You know, the noble Sir Galahad on the quest for the Holy Grail, slaying dragons, rescuing damsels in distress, and all that. We generally dismiss virtue as an archaic ideal and hardly expect it from ourselves or others.

Yet Lao Tse believes:

Those who follow the Tao
Are at one with the Tao.
Those who are virtuous
Experience Virtue.
Those who lose their way
Are lost.
When you are at one with the Tao,
The Tao welcomes you.
When you are at one with Virtue,
Virtue is always there.

— 23

Could it be that virtue is real and precious, and can make the difference between a difficult life and one that shines? Might the ills of our society exist because we have lost sight of integrity and allowed hypocrisy to seize normality? We have so few role models of noble character that dignity has become the exception rather than the rule. We expect politicians to serve special interests rather than their constituents, and we hardly bat an eye when their sex or graft scandals hit the news. We are not surprised when Manhattan apartment dwellers have three locks and a reinforcement bar behind their front door to keep out intruders. We feed our kids foods filled with empty ingredients, sugar, and chemicals, and then we wonder why they are hyperactive, bipolar, and diabetic. Then they spend their days and nights glued to screens and depend on thumbs to communicate. We put up with having to practically undress before we are allowed to ride on an airplane. We don't question our values when crazed shoppers trample pregnant women to death as hordes charge through superstores at 5 A.M. on Black Friday. When we hear about another mass shooting, we are numbed rather than outraged. *It's just the way life is these days*, we tell ourselves, and press a button on the remote to watch the game of the week.

A culture with a sense of virtue would not get into such a mess, and if it did, would not long tolerate it. The only reason we put up with despicable conditions is that we do not believe that better ones are available. Lao Tse would call us to a higher vision. He would say that the Tao that created heaven and earth and all that is good is available to us. *Tao Te Ching* is the hand of grace reaching into a writhing humanity to rescue it from the ills we have created when we turned our backs on love.

If there is a good store of Virtue,
then nothing is impossible.
If nothing is impossible, then there are no limits.
If we know no limits, then we are fit to rule.
The mother principle of ruling holds good
for a long time.
This is called having deep roots and a firm foundation,
The Tao of long life and eternal vision.
—— 59

What Makes Life Work

A life of virtue is like a majestic temple upheld by 12 sturdy columns. As you establish these pillars as the mainstays of your life, you will experience deep soul satisfaction and attain brilliant success. But you must first understand how each pillar achieves its holding power. Let us now tour the temple and discover what makes it mighty.

1. Honesty means trusting that the truth is your friend and it will take you where you want and need to go. It is said, "The truth hurts," but the only thing the truth hurts is illusions. Ultimately the truth heals. One of my coaching clients confessed to me that she had been having an affair and she planned to tell her husband. When she did, he admitted that he had secretly been a cocaine addict. Their truth-telling session brought to the surface a cesspool of hidden material that had been sucking life force from their relationship. The more the couple revealed themselves to each other, the more bonded they felt. My client ended her affair and her husband quit using drugs. While telling the truth was uncomfortable and scary for both of them, it saved their marriage.

This is not to guarantee that if you tell your partner the truth it will save your marriage. Sometimes it will end your marriage. But how much of a marriage do you have if you have to lie to keep it?

If you are committed to success, you can find a way to tell the truth in a loving way. I have had to end relationships, fire employees, and evict tenants, and I have found that when I keep respect and positive intention as the foundation of the conversation, the interaction usually goes well and the change works out in everyone's best interest. Some people pride themselves on being brutally honest, but, as Canadian humorist Richard J. Needham noted, "People who are brutally honest get more satisfaction out of the brutality than out of the honesty." Authentic honesty is kind, healing, and liberating.

Is lying ever justified? Only when it will serve a greater good. In an earlier chapter I told about the imposter aeronautical engineer who calmed a frantic airplane passenger by assuring her the aircraft would not crash. Now let's consider a situation where an outright lie in disregard of man-made law would be an expression of the Tao. Imagine that you lived in Germany during the Nazi regime, and a Jewish couple came to you for asylum. Out of compassion you let them stay with you and you hide them. The next day a Nazi official pounds on your door and asks if you have seen these people. What, in this case, would be the way of the Tao? Would it be more ethical to uphold government laws based on fear, racism, hatred, and genocide, or to save the lives of innocent human beings? I like to think that you or I would choose the latter. When human law is not founded in the Tao, what is spiritually legal supersedes what is politically legal.

Honesty means living true to the Great Way. When people make laws that contradict the laws of spirit, you are being dishonest to follow human laws. *A Course in Miracles* asks us to remember, "I am under no laws but God's."

2. Integrity means that the life you are living on the outside matches who you are on the inside. It does not mean that you stuff yourself into a code of ethics imposed upon you by some external source. Lao Tse calls such a condition "morality," and he does not have a lot of good things to say about it. There is a place inside every human being that knows what is right. Oppressive governments, religions, families, and societies deny that individuals are capable of governing their own lives, so every aspect of their activity must be dictated and controlled by the institution. At a primal level, this may be appropriate. When people have lost touch with their internal guidance, they must be told how to live. But if you are reading this book, you have likely evolved past that primitive stage and you are capable of differentiating right from wrong by consulting your inner knowing. My teacher used to say, "Religion teaches obedience. Spirituality teaches self-discipline." There comes a time when you cease to look outward for answers and you start to look within. Such a day is a milestone on your spiritual journey and should be regarded with humility, awe, and a sense of adventure.

The amount of pain in your life is in direct proportion to the size of the gap between who you are and how you are living. The greater the gap, the more frustration, conflict, and depression. The smaller the gap, the more vitality, creativity, and inner peace. The size of that gap is entirely up to you. People or organizations can try to control you, but you are fully in charge of how much the life you are living reflects your true self. Lao Tse would urge you to take time each day to assess your walk and determine whether or not you are in integrity with yourself. If you are, carry on. If not, make the changes necessary to be more of who you were born to be.

If I have even just a little sense,
I will walk on the main road

and my only fear will be of straying from it.

— 53

3. Kindness is the telling characteristic of spiritual evolution. Jewish theologian Abraham Joshua Heschel said, "When I was young, I admired clever people. Now that I am old, I admire kind people." Any expression of mean-spiritedness or cruelty is a sign that you are in pain and you are attempting to relieve yourself of your discomfort by passing it along to others. But this never works. Gandhi said, "'An eye for an eye and a tooth for a tooth' leaves the entire world blind and toothless." Kindness is the redemption of humanity. The world is in the mess we observe because we feel separate and alone. Kindness bridges that gap and dissolves alienation. World peace will never come about by conquering nations. It will come only by conquering the dark aspects of ourselves and replacing domination with compassion.

I believe that the only true religion consists
of having a good heart.

— His Holiness the Dalai Lama

On our way home from Youli, we passed through a village where we encountered a starving dog. The poor creature was emaciated, little more than skin and bones. Weak and frail, the dog was lying on its side beside a small house, panting heavily. People were passing by, hardly paying attention to the animal.

"Excuse me," the master interrupted one fellow. "Does anyone care for this dog?"

The man replied, "That dog belonged to Sheng Wei. He said it is possessed by a devil. It should be left to die."

The master's face tightened. "The Tao does not give its power to devils," he replied. "It cares for all of its creatures like a mother loves her children."

The man walked on, unfazed. Lao Tse reached into the pack on his bamboo stick and took out a bowl. Then he went door to door in the village and, as if begging for himself, received donations of food. Half an hour later he returned to the dog and gave it a generous helping, which it devoured ravenously. Soon a bit of strength returned to its fragile form.

Then the master took a sash out of his pack, fashioned a sling, and wrapped the cloth over his shoulders and chest. He motioned to me to pick up the dog, and I placed it in the sling. Then he wrapped the fabric around the animal so he could carry it without using his hands.

"We will not leave you here to die," he told the dog. "You are coming home with us, where devils created by fearful men have no reality."

We walked on. After a while I took the dog, and for the remainder of the journey we took turns carrying the creature.

When we arrived home the master gave the dog a good meal. Tears came to my eyes as I watched it eat so gratefully. "I think we will call you 'Full,'" said Lao Tse. "Your stomach is now full and the Tao provides for you without reservation."

I will never forget the look in Full's eyes. She was so happy.

Full stayed with the master, constantly by his side, for the rest of her life. She never missed a meal again.

[The Great Way] covers all creatures like the sky,

but does not dominate them . . .

The sage imitates this conduct . . .

— 34

4. Embracing all elevates a society from "Me first" to "We're all in this together." During the first session of my retreats for Japanese students, I ask each person to declare their intention for themselves for the week, and their prayer for the group. Even though I instruct the participants to state their intentions in that order (a product of my Western culture mind-set) they always state their prayer for the group first and their personal intention second.

A fascinating study published in the journal *Behavioral and Brain Sciences* revealed striking differences between "individualistic" and "collectivistic" mind-sets. Western cultures tend to think, *What's in it for me?* while Eastern cultures ask, "How can I help?" Westerners tend to blame, while Easterners are more concerned with compassion. Dr. Shinobu Kitayama at the University of Michigan asked a group of Western-thinkers and a group of Eastern-thinkers to each comment on the situation of a baseball player taking performance-enhancing drugs. The Westerners focused on content and tended to fault the player for defective character. The Easterners focused more on context and considered that the player may have been subject to societal pressure to perform.

These two disparate mind-sets represent the difference between separatist thinking and holistic thinking. People of virtue think beyond personal interests and consider how their actions affect the whole. They are less concerned with what they can get for themselves, and more concerned with how they can contribute to the community.

> *Know the strength of a man,*
> *But keep a woman's care!*
> *Be the stream of the universe!*
> *Being the stream of the universe,*
> *Ever true and unswerving,*
> *Become as a little child once more.*
>
> —— 28

5. Keeping your word stabilizes relationships and commerce, and honors those with whom you interact. In his landmark book *The Four Agreements*, Don Miguel Ruiz advises, "Be impeccable with your word." If you say you are going to do something, do it. If you make a plan, follow through. If you schedule an appointment, show up on time. If you borrow money, pay it back. If you are not sure you can do something, don't promise it. The Bible tells us, "Let your 'yes' be a 'yes' and your 'no' be a 'no.' All else is the work of the devil." Don't allow fear, resistance, vagueness, or ancillary details to sidetrack you. Develop a reputation that you are dependable. In Yiddish, the word *mensch* means "a person of good character." Be a mensch and set in motion a string of good karma that will bless you and those you touch. Being true to your word will leave a legacy of respect, harmonious relations, and personal and professional success.

In dealing with others, be gentle and kind.

In speech, be true.

— 8

6. Generosity demonstrates that you know you live in an abundant universe capable of providing for all of your needs and those of everyone. You do not fear to give because you recognize that the Tao is the source of infinite supply. Generosity does not apply only to money and material things; it is more about your spirit. You do not have to be financially wealthy to be generous. You can give love, kindness, time, listening, patience, caring, appreciation, compliments, and service. When in doubt, give. It is said, "You cannot outgive God," meaning that there is no end to the resources at your disposal. When you know you are heir to the riches of the universe, you can share them liberally without fear of loss or depletion. You are entitled to *all* of the kingdom, and when you welcome others to join you there, you strengthen your residency.

Who has more than enough and gives it to the world?

Only the wise.

—— 77

7. **Patience** is one of the most valuable virtues we can cultivate in a lightning-speed world. *A Course in Miracles* tells us, "Patience is natural to those who trust." Impatience means that you see yourself as deprived or needy and you are itching for something better than what is here. Yet all the riches you seek are right where you stand. *A Course in Miracles* asks us to remember, "I am content to be wherever He wishes, knowing He goes there with me." In Hermann Hesse's novel *Siddhartha*, the man who is to become the Buddha declares that he has mastered three traits of character: "I can think. I can fast. I can wait." In a push-button culture we expect everything to occur immediately. When it does not, we get frustrated and we complain. When the Internet was first developed, connection and download speeds were slower than they are now. It took maybe 15 seconds to get online, and a little while for pages to download. I remember hearing someone in my office dub the Internet "the Worldwide Wait." I scratched my head. We now have a miraculous technology that allows us to communicate with just about anyone around the world instantly and gain access to the entire database of human knowledge at the touch of a finger. Not long ago if you were going to conduct research for a project, you would have to go to a library and plod through the shelves for obscure books, or send away for one and wait for it to be mailed, or possibly travel to a distant city or country to look up records. You might have to interview someone that would require months of correspondence to set up, as well as travel time and expense. Now messages flash across the globe in a nanosecond and you can enjoy a video interaction with someone halfway around the globe for free by simply pressing a few keys. What not long ago would have taken months, years, or a lifetime can now be achieved in a matter of moments. And you are complaining about having to wait 30 seconds for a web page to download?

Patience has been one of my life lessons to master. I want it all now. I do not like to wait in lines or traffic, or for people who are late for meetings. One technique that has helped me has been to use my waiting time wisely rather than just get frustrated. So while in line at the post office, I strike up a conversation with someone near me, practice my, *A Course in Miracles* lesson, think about the content of a book I am working on, or wave to a child. While on hold on the phone, I check e-mail, file some papers, or clean my desk. While in traffic I listen to music or an inspirational audio. There is always something I can do more interesting than waiting for something better to happen, some way I can use my mind productively. I am responsible for my experience, and I do not give that sacred power to the postal clerk or tech support agent. French naturalist Jules Renard said, "I am never bored anywhere. Boredom is an affront to oneself."

Impatience means that you do not trust the Tao to deliver what you need when you need it. Patience means that you have faith that the Tao is with you right where you stand. One of my favorite affirmations is "God's timing is perfect."

The quality of your life depends not on what your body is doing, but on where you place your mind. It is possible to be in physically undesirable circumstances and establish your mind in an expansive domain. It is also possible to be in a physically ideal situation and have your mind be imprisoned in a dungeon of fear. Our ultimate power lives in the mind. When we use our mind to appreciate what is before us, everything unfolds perfectly.

Adopt the pace of nature: her secret is patience.
— RALPH WALDO EMERSON

8. Gratitude is the door through which you reach the riches you seek. The happiest people are those who say "Thank you" the most. My mentor said, "You need to thank me. Not because I need your thanks, but because you need to give it." It has been said, "There are so many men who can figure costs, and so few who can measure values."

Complaint is the antithesis of gratitude. Should you be tempted to complain, find something to be grateful for instead. A comedian recounted that he was on an airplane when the in-flight entertainment system stopped working for a few minutes. The passenger seated next to him grunted, "Doesn't anything work anymore?" The comedian thought to himself, *Here you are sitting in a chair in a meticulously engineered aircraft traveling nearly 600 miles an hour at an altitude of 35,000 feet. You are speeding from Atlanta to San Francisco in five hours, a trip that once would have taken a year, which you might not have survived. You are being served a hot meal with wine while using Wi-Fi to surf the Web, send e-mail, and text your kids. When the entertainment system comes back on in a few minutes, you will have your choice of a hundred movies and as many music and educational channels. You can get up and go to the bathroom anytime you like. Every modern comfort, convenience, and safety is provided for you during your journey. And you say, "Nothing is working?"*

The truth is that far, far, far more things work than don't work. Most things work almost all the time. What is not working are our thoughts that deny all the good things that are working. Even when things don't appear to be working, the challenge is bringing us some insight that will help us as we overcome it. In that sense, everything is working. The master of the Tao makes everything work in her favor by recognizing, receiving, celebrating, and expanding the blessings already present.

Surrender yourself humbly; then you can be trusted to care for all things.

Love the world as your own self; then you can truly care for all things.

— 13

9. Presence makes the crucial difference in human interactions. In a world in which many people have given their presence and power away to busyness and technology, fully being with another person is more important than ever.

In my Life Coach Training Program, "The Power of Presence" is one of the first lessons students receive. When a coach is genuinely present with a client; or teacher with student; parent with child; doctor with patient; manager with employee; or salesperson with customer, you establish the platform for success. If someone is in pain or has a pressing need, they want you to help them bridge a gap. Being fully with that person is the first step to filling that gap. These days people do not simply crave presence. They are *starving* for it. To be present with another human being is to feed their soul—and yours.

One of my coach graduates has held a longtime position as the complaint department at a public power company. Whenever a customer has a problem, Linda is the first one to hear about it. When she entered coach training, Linda was about to quit her job, burned out from 10 years of trying to satisfy disgruntled customers. In the training, Linda learned the skills of reflective listening, giving the customer her full attention, demonstrating that she has heard their communication, and empathizing with their feelings. Linda reframed her job as an opportunity to show up with her clients and support them energetically as well as logistically. After a few months of implementing these new skills, she told me, "I love my job now! I have no desire to leave. I so enjoy connecting with our customers and developing relationships with them. When I give them my full presence, I receive as much as they do." A corporate customer relations motto captures the ideal scenario: "The customer is not an interruption of our work—he is the purpose of it."

If I were to ask you, "Which teachers or mentors have had the greatest impact on your life, and why?" you would probably not cite those who taught you the most facts. You would more likely remember the teachers who gave you their undivided attention, looked you in the eye, cared for you as a person, saw goodness or greatness in you, and inspired you to be all you could be. I remember some of what I learned in high school and a little more of what I learned in college. Mostly I remember the teachers who believed in me and connected with me not just as a student but as a friend; who saw me not just as the object of their job, but as a person with potential they could draw forth.

Each day you and I have a thousand opportunities to be present or not. Stepping away from your computer when your child needs your help; sitting quietly, holding the hand of an aging parent; or kindly repeating for your client an answer you have already given him. These are the fibers that build the nest of life. What we often consider "menial" human interactions are quite significant: asking the clerk at your corner convenience store how his kid is doing; waving at the workman guiding traffic around a construction zone; thanking the hotel chambermaid for the extra cleaning she did. These "little" acts of connection are not little at all; they make the difference between a day plodded through and a day of genuine reward. Robert Brault suggested, "Do not call any work menial until you have watched a proud person do it."

I saw a funny hidden video camera gag in which an actress sat on a park bench next to a stranger. The actress feigned falling asleep and rested her head on the stranger's shoulder. Different strangers displayed a variety of reactions. In some cases the stranger woke the girl up and walked away. In other cases the person figured, *This girl needs to get some rest,* and allowed her to sleep on his or her shoulder. We always have the choice between being present with another person or not.

I felt it shelter to speak to you.

— EMILY DICKINSON

10. Claiming **self-reliance** represents one of the most significant turning points in a human being's evolution. It signals the crucial shift from dependence on outer authority to reliance on inner knowing. From infancy you were taught that people outside you know more about how you should live than you know. Parents, elder siblings, teachers, priests, and the government were supposedly all smarter than you; if you want to be happy and successful, you must listen to what they tell you to do.

Eventually each of us comes to the point where we realize that how we were taught to live is not the way we were born to live. Mega-successful British playwright Tom Stoppard wrote, "It's the best possible time to be alive, when almost everything you thought you knew is wrong!" At a crucial instant each of us starts trusting our inner guidance more than others' opinions or directives. Facing this crossroad can be frightening, as it may call us to make changes in our life that others might not approve of. You may even have to reinvent yourself. Yet it is liberating to recognize that you have more choices and freedom than you realized. Such a moment marks the beginning of your true spiritual path.

The Tao cannot be prescribed for you. It must emerge from within you. You will not master your life by pleasing others. You will master it by aligning with yourself. The God that you have been taught is out there somewhere, is in here. External temples are reflections of the inner sanctuary. If they do their job properly, they will lead you home to yourself. If they lead you elsewhere, run like hell. Giving your power away to an external source *is* hell. Finding it within you is heaven.

11. Let us now shed more light on the virtue of **humility**. Humble people are confident because they recognize the Tao is the source of their good. The ego resists humility like the plague because it implies there is a greater wisdom than the ego's plan. So the ego threatens that if you humbled yourself you would be annihilated. But the truth is that if you humbled yourself you would be exhilarated.

There are two aspects of humility we need to put into practice. One is to renounce arrogance, ostentation, and attempts to manipulate people and force things to go the way we think they should. It means letting go of obsessive control and the need to be right. This is difficult for many of us. We believe that we can squeeze success out of the universe by manhandling people and events. But if we can let go of our need to be in the driver's seat, deep inner quietude follows, along with miraculous outcomes.

Tao Te Ching is the world's most potent antidote for control freaks. We can relax, breathe, and allow life to unfold in our favor. When we renounce our demands on the world, we gain the freedom and peace that we hoped constant control would bring us, but never does.

> *[The great Tao] does not show greatness,*
> *And is therefore truly great.*
>
> — 34

The second aspect of humility calls us to accept our gifts and express them. You acknowledge your talents, passions, and visions, and you act on them with confidence and even boldness. To say or imply, "I am unworthy," is not a statement of humility. It is an assertion of arrogance as you deny that the Tao created you with deep intrinsic value. You are here for a purpose and must do your part to manifest your destiny. Do not fall into the trap of believing you are unqualified and you do not deserve to achieve meaningful results or have good things for yourself. Such self-negation is a denial of your identity and calling. It is possible to do great things and remain humble. Some of the most luminary individuals in recent history have remained humble while moving mountains. Game changers like Barack Obama, Meryl Streep, and Elon Musk have carried huge, high-profile torches in industries in which most of their peers have fallen prey to the trappings of riches, fame, power, and ego. But these individuals have kept service above selfishness, and as a result have engendered massive achievements that have improved the lives of many millions.

Humility is not about playing small. It is about putting the smallness of the human personality aside to make way for the greatness of the Tao to shine.

Know honor,
Yet remain humble.
Be the valley of the universe!
Being the valley of the universe,
Ever true and resourceful,
Return to the state of the uncarved block.

—— 28

12. Vision enables spiritual masters—please include yourself in this group—to see beyond appearances into loftier possibilities. If you accept what is as all that could be, what is becomes what will be. Part of you recognizes that any form of lack or limitation is not the ultimate truth, and you yearn for a better way. You cannot simultaneously bow to the limited and dwell in the infinite. "A man cannot serve two masters. He will love the one and hate the other, or he will hate the one and love the other." This is a metaphor for the distinction you and I must make daily: Is the world of fear, separation, decay, and death the true reality, or is there a more glorious dimension in which we can abide?

Master healers, teachers, and world-change agents see their clients, students, and society as greater than those recipients see themselves. They focus on what is working or what could work rather than apparent deficits.

I am good to people who are good.
I am also good to people who are not good,
Because Virtue is goodness.
I have faith in people who are faithful.
I also have faith in people who are not faithful,
Because Virtue is faithfulness.

— 81

In Alejandro Jodorowsky's bizarrely brilliant film *The Holy Mountain*, a spiritual master sets up a target, gives his student a dart, and tells him, "When the bull's-eye becomes as big in your mind as an elephant, you are sure to hit it." We must fill our mind with stirring possibilities and desired outcomes so that lesser scenarios have no room left to occupy our consciousness. A visionary does not create great things happening. He sees great things as *already* happening, and steps into them because they are already so.

Your temple of virtue is firmly established and calls you to dwell in it. This temple does not require you to offer sacrifices, but rather to walk in dignity. The only sacrifice required is that of fear. While the fogs of human malice and cultural compromise have obscured the temple of virtue from view, the pillars have not been marred. As you approach, they gleam with the purity in which they were cast. Be not deceived by those who appear to thrive by amassing power, fame, and worldly accolades. These are but cheap trinkets, glittering toys to distract and amuse the unawakened. You have a different purpose. You are here to manifest a higher reward. The good things of the world will come to you not because you seek them, but as by-products of your intention to live in the light. Do not apologize for speaking the word *virtue* and striving to live it. In the end, that is all that will matter.

Everyone under heaven says that my Tao is great
and beyond compare.

Because it is great, it seems different.

If it were not different, it would have vanished long ago.

— 67

The Tao alone nourishes
And brings everything to fulfillment.

— 41

WHAT'S LEFT
TO LEARN

*In the pursuit of learning, something is
acquired every day.
In the pursuit of the Tao, every day
something is relinquished.*

— 48

The Gospel of Thomas is one of the ancient manuscripts
that make up the Nag Hammadi Library discovered in upper
Egypt in 1945. Written soon after Jesus walked the earth, the
text contains aphorisms astoundingly similar to *Tao Te Ching*. In
that gospel, Thomas says,

> *If you bring forth what is within you,*
> *what you bring forth will save you.*
> *If you do not bring forth what is within you,*
> *what you do not bring forth will destroy you.*

The world would have you believe that success is achieved
by amassing knowledge. The Tao would have you believe that
success is achieved by accessing wisdom. The world teaches that
answers are somewhere out there and you need to import them.
The Tao teaches that answers are in here and you need to draw
them forth. The world insists that the person armed with the
most facts wields the most power. The Tao suggests that the

person most aligned with the Great Way has the strength of the universe at his fingertips.

Many people pursue training after training because they believe that if they just get enough certificates and degrees, one day they will be qualified. If you follow this path, there is always a gap between what you know and what you should know. Because that gap is born of a false sense of inadequacy, it is never filled. Something deep inside is missing and no matter how many more courses you take, how many diplomas you hang on your wall, and how many letters you list after you name, an insatiable void disquiets your gut.

Lao Tse sees education and enlightenment from a different perspective. He would say that you are not here to learn something you do not know. You are here to remember what you already know. The spiritual path is not a learning curve. It is a refresher course. You were born knowing. Then you were educated out of knowing. Now you need to be reeducated into remembering. The journey of enlightenment is not one of doing. It is of *undoing*. You must undo the debilitating illusions that have been laid over your majestic self. The goal of living is to become what you already are.

Yet in a world severely handicapped with endless layers of illusory need, demand for more, nonessential accoutrements, social posturing, brutal competition, quest to impress, and obsessive image management, it is a rare person who can throw off decades of armoring and breathe the fresh air of innocent self-confidence. Lao Tse urges us to beware the misuse of education as a distraction from awakening or a cave in which to hide from life. He would have us peel away what has been laid over us like an ill-fitting garment, and trust that our natural self will succeed far more gloriously than our invented self.

Genuine teachers rescue you from the nightmare of trying to stuff yourself into tiny boxes that insult your magnitude, and cheer you on to walk your passionate path. The Tao would free you from the endless accumulation of facts that clutter your brain with trivia, and instead reward you for revealing your inherent brilliance. Thus your education shifts from climbing a mountain of data to reach a summit without a view, to stripping away the blinders that blocked the sweeping vista you were missing.

Give up learning, and put an end to your troubles.

—— 20

On a misty morning when the clouds kissed the earth, I could make out Lao Tse's figure as he was arriving back at his cottage from his morning walk. He was wearing his conical coolie hat and thick gray robe that made him almost dissolve into the shroud of fog.

"Master," I called out in a loud voice that would have startled another man. Yet Lao Tse took my noise in stride as if hearing two birds fighting in a distant tree. He waved silently.

"Have you heard the news?" I asked as I approached, almost out of breath.

He surveyed my eyes and awaited my report.

"You know Chou Huo, the headmaster at the Imperial College?"

"Yes, I met him a few times."

"They found him dead this morning. He committed suicide by eating a mass of salt."

Lao Tse nodded pensively and looked off into the distance, as if conferring with some invisible spirit. He took a breath and placed his hand at my lower back. "Let's talk about this," he said as he guided me toward the cabin.

Once inside, I took a seat while the master lit a fire and set a pot of water over it. Silently he tidied some vegetables on a counter. Sometimes he would put objects in order as if he were rearranging the world. I knew him well enough not to press him to speak. He would offer words when the time was right. Finally the water reached boiling and he crumbled tea leaves into the pot. Soon a pungent minty aroma wafted my way. "Chou Huo was your teacher at one time, wasn't he?"

"Yes, that is why I am so upset," I answered, eager to air my feelings. "He was an excellent teacher, respected by students and his colleagues. Chou Huo was praised throughout the province. He had even been called to one of the emperor's ministers as a consultant. He was the last person I expected would ever commit suicide."

The master leaned over and glanced into the pot of water. Not steeped enough yet. "Then why do you think he killed himself?"

"People are saying he had a stormy family life. His wife would not obey him and his children were doing poorly in school. He felt ashamed and drank a lot. On the morning before his demise, his eldest son was suspended from school for making fun of his teacher in public."

The master looked at me squarely. "Do you believe that what people are saying is so?"

I nodded. "I think it is. When Chou Huo was my teacher he took a great deal of pride in his position. He cited little-known facts that made him stand out, and often compared himself favorably to other instructors. He labored to protect his reputation. I believe his shame around his family was too much for him to bear."

By now the tea was ready and the master poured me a cup. As I held the mug between my hands, the warmth offset the chill of the morning.

"What can you learn from this?"

"I remember you telling me, 'Everyone is your teacher. Some teach you what to do and others teach you what not to do.' In this case I believe that Chou Huo's downfall was his pride. His entire world was built on his public image. When that was stained, he could not accept the embarrassment."

Lao Tse sat beside me. "You may be correct." He stared into his teacup for a moment, as if fishing a truth from its depth. "I think there is also a deeper lesson."

"What is that?"

"Facts and knowledge do not yield happiness. Here was a man who knew more facts than almost everyone else, and he was also more miserable than almost everyone else. He had amassed a great deal of information, but he did not know how to live."

Of course. In retrospect, that seemed clear.

> "The Tao is not concerned with facts," he went on. "Anyone can learn what is taught in the classroom. Many students pass their exams simply by parroting words from a book or teacher. But ideas by themselves cannot substitute for experience. The realm of intellect is just a portion of life. Far fewer people have mastered the kingdom of the heart. That is what the Tao would teach you."
>
> I sipped my tea slowly as I considered the tragic death of a man the world honored, but who could not honor himself. I said a silent prayer for his soul and asked that I found my life in character rather than knowledge.

Those who know are not learned.

The learned do not know.

—— 81

The Missing Vitamin

Our public educational system has faltered in important ways for several reasons: (1) Much of what students are taught is irrelevant to their lives; (2) Students are trained to fit into societal molds rather than being rewarded for their unique passions and talents; (3) Teachers and administrators are overwhelmed by a mountain of fear-based regulations and paperwork that stifle creative expression; and (4) The system does not address or much care for the lives of the students outside the classroom, which exert a far more profound effect on their education than what happens during the school day.

My client Ron complained that his 16-year-old daughter was not doing well in school. She was missing classes and getting poor grades. As a result, the girl's parents tried to pressure her into academic excellence, which led to an ongoing fight within their household.

"What does your daughter like to do?" I asked Ron.

"She loves art. In all of her free time she airbrushes T-shirts." Ron took out his phone and showed me a photo of one of her creations. I was floored! The art piece was uniquely creative and quite professional. The girl was obviously talented. "I suggest you give up trying to turn your artistically gifted daughter into a scholar, and get behind her to do what she loves and what she is good at," I told him. "This young lady can easily create a successful and spiritually rewarding career as an artist. If you let her be what she is, the fights will end and you will all thrive." He was open to my suggestion and he agreed to support his daughter in her art.

A few months later Ron brought his daughter to one of my lectures. She was a radiant spirit, wearing one of her T-shirts. She thanked me for asking her parents to support her. Her art was flourishing and she was happy. I told her I knew she would do very well. Tears came to her eyes.

The young lady was just waiting for someone to affirm her. That was the vitamin her soul needed, the one we all require. When we miss it, we starve. When we receive or give it, we thrive.

Student-Sourced Education

There are many fine schools that draw forth students' talents, and many dedicated teachers who make a difference in their students' lives. Good schools serve a crucial purpose. Yet in many ways we are still stuck in the paradigm that education occurs from the outside in, rather than from the inside out; that students are empty and must be filled rather than that they are whole and must be encouraged to express. What good is it if you receive accolades for passing academic tests when you have lost your soul along the way?

In response to public education not meeting the deeper needs of many students, numerous alternative models have developed. One of them is the Sudbury school, which bases education on what students are motivated to learn. Students are simply asked to show up for school and let the teachers know what curriculum would be meaningful to them. If a student wants to learn how to play the saxophone, a saxophone teacher will be brought in. If the student wishes to climb a tree for the morning, that is his education that day. If a child is not interested in learning to read at age five, the school will wait until she reaches age seven or eight and asks for reading help. Learning is guided by students' passion and intention rather than an imposed curriculum.

While many people might contend that such a curriculum is too lackadaisical or permissive, the results speak to the contrary: 87 percent of Sudbury graduates go on to college or another institution of higher learning. In many ways this radical alternative system works better than traditional models. I wonder what would happen if we changed public-school rules so that only students and teachers who want to be in school would have to be there. How many would actually show up? Probably only a small portion of those there now. It's extremely difficult to teach people who are not motivated to learn, by teachers who would rather be elsewhere. The breakdown in current institutions, including education, moves us to consider alternatives based on inspiration and vision rather than rote models based on compulsion and competition.

Education is not filling a pail
but the lighting of a fire.
— WILLIAM BUTLER YEATS

My friend Marty is a developmentally challenged fellow in his late teens; his mentality has been assessed as that of an eight-year-old. Marty's reading skills are poor, and when his parents gave him a computer he ignored it. Instead, he enjoys watching "professional" wrestling on television. He knows all the wrestlers, who are the good guys and who are the villains, and he cheers for his favorites. Recently Marty became enamored with a sexy female wrestler. When he found out that she had a fan club he could join online, Marty went to the computer and miraculously learned how to use it. I find it fascinating that until that day, his parents and counselors believed he was not smart enough to learn how to use a computer. But when he had a good reason, he "became" smart enough.

We are all smart enough to do what we value doing. We find the time, money, and means to achieve what is important to us. We are not motivated to do the things that other people tell us we should do or we should want to do. Passion is the hand of the Tao reaching into the world to get things done. When you are excited about reaching a goal, you are connected to the source of life. Many people judge or dismiss passion as being self-indulgent, but authentic passion moves us to fulfill our soul's mission, attract abundance and success, *and* serve humanity. When you express your true delight, you make the world a better place. If you squash your passion, you are trying to repress the Tao, which always backfires. If your life is not working, a little or a lot, tell the truth about how you feel about what you are doing, and what you would rather be doing. In that one honest statement you take a major step to reclaim the Tao.

Children in indigenous cultures were exposed to all the aspects of the community and encouraged to explore what they felt drawn to. If you were a child fascinated by boats, you would spend your days with the outrigger builder, watching and helping him. If you liked cloth design, you would go to the hut of the village weaver and learn from her. If hunting excited you, you would foray into the jungle with the hunters. Instead of prescribing a life path for their children, parents would observe the life path the children were attracted to and encourage them to follow that. This is the way masters develop.

Lao Tse would have us rethink our priorities. He would encourage us to pursue well-being above social obligation. He understood that when we are happy we are in alignment with the Tao, and our vitality automatically spills to everyone and everything we touch.

More words count less.
Hold fast to the center.
—— 5

From Student to Master

Nearly all educational, religious, and philosophical belief systems define us as students in the school of life. I have heard many people declare, "I am a lifelong learner." When we adopt this identity, we assume we are here to face and master more and more lessons until we graduate. But, as you may have noticed, graduation never comes in this lifetime. Your learning curve is so steep that you will have to come back for many lifetimes to master all of your lessons. You are not just a lifelong learner. You are in this for eons, and you may never get off the wheel of karma.

Everything you have taught yourself has made your
power more and more obscure to you.
— A Course in Miracles

I ask you now to consider a radical, even heretical vision: What if we defined ourselves not as learners, but as knowers; not seekers, but finders; not students, but masters? What if you were born knowing, and you have simply forgotten what you knew when you arrived? What if the notion of being a soul that needs to continually reincarnate to keep learning endlessly is a distraction from the wholeness you already embody? When a female child is born, she already contains within her all the eggs she will either pass or have fertilized as an adult. All that she can bring into the world is already a part of her. A woman does not grow or import new eggs. Likewise, we all come into the world carrying the potential for all we can be.

Seeking is an activity of the ego. Finding is an activity of the spirit. Most people identify themselves as seekers. We seek a mate, car, house, or job. Eventually we seek truth, healing, and enlightenment. We are continually reaching for something out there, something we are missing, something we do not already own, some elusive commodity that someone or something will give us. Education as we know it is a form of seeking. Enlightenment is a form of finding. *A Course in Miracles* tells us, "Enlightenment is but a recognition, not a change at all." T. S. Eliot eloquently stated, "The end of all our exploring will be to arrive where we started and know the place for the first time."

I invite you to take the unthinkable step of giving up learning. Quit seeking for more of anything, including education, and establish yourself in the wisdom seeded within you. Attend a school or get a degree, or many, if you wish—not because the training will fill your emptiness, but because it will give you a venue to express your aliveness. Proceed from joy rather than need.

Give up your lust for growth.

— WHITE EAGLE

If you renounce your identity as a student, your education will occur as a natural by-product of your journey rather than the goal. This is the consciousness that Lao Tse and other great masters attained and would have you share. Enlightened beings realize that they had it all the time. What is in them is also in you. They don't want you to follow them as icons; they want you to emulate them by stepping into your own strength. Then and only then will you graduate from the school of life, which is not a school at all, but a place to discover the brilliant light you are and the gifts you came to give.

Without going outside, you may know the whole world.

Without looking through the window, you may
see the ways of heaven.

The farther you go, the less you know.

Thus the wise know without traveling;

See without looking;

Work without doing.

—— 47

THE GREAT
BALANCING ACT

Therefore the wise avoid extremes, excesses,
and complacency.

— 29

While Lao Tse was bringing the Tao to China, not far away in India young Prince Siddhartha was growing up in an opulent castle where he enjoyed all the luxuries of royalty. In his stately enclave he was shielded from the pain of the world. Then one day he ventured beyond the castle walls and for the first time he saw people poor, sick, old, and dying. This rocked Siddhartha's world and spurred him on to an intense spiritual quest to know why suffering exists and how to relieve it.

The renunciate prince swung to another extreme and for many years practiced mortifying his flesh. He denied his body by eating one grain of rice per day; walking barefoot; sitting nearly naked in bitter cold; standing on one foot; and sleeping on nails. As a result of his austerities, Siddhartha became sick and emaciated. Then a woman took pity on him and offered him a bowl of rice pudding. While in his ascetic practice Siddhartha would have refused, in that moment he decided to accept. We are told that was the turning point at which the renunciate prince became the enlightened Buddha. He recognized that all the elements of life exist for a purpose, and we must live in harmony with ourselves and our environment. We must embrace our humanity, not resist it. He then taught the importance of walking "the middle path"—a life of moderation and balance.

Lao Tse came to the same realization. He cautioned against excesses and extremes, and advised us to live with equilibrium. The famous yin-yang symbol of Taoism captures this principle, illustrating the existence of opposites and our need to integrate them: light and dark, life and death, male and female, good and evil, joy and pain. To deny opposites sets us up for suffering. To recognize them and make them work on our behalf yields mastery.

Too much of anything, the master taught, is no good. Too little of anything is no good. We must each find our "sweet spot," the just-right integration of contrasting elements that, when we step into it, makes us both happy and productive.

One day as winter approached, the master went into the village, leaving me to tend his cabin. I decided to surprise him by chopping firewood, so I found his axe and began hacking at trees. I pushed on through the day, and by late afternoon I was exhausted. My back hurt, I had blisters on my hands, and I started to cough. But at least I had completed my mission to help my teacher.

When Lao Tse returned just before sunset, he was very pleased with all that I had done. He thanked me profusely and told me to come in and have a bath and dinner. But by the time the meal came, I felt so tired and weak that I could not even eat. My cough aggravated and I had to go lie down.

The master sat beside me on my bed and looked at me with pity. He placed his hand on my forehead to feel my temperature. "You worked too hard today."

"I wanted to finish the job before you came home," I explained.

"That was very kind of you. But you ran your health down. That is not the way of the Tao."

Somehow it always came back to that.

"At what point did you start to feel very tired?"

I scanned my memory. "It was midafternoon. I started to sweat a lot and my knees felt wobbly."

"Then that is the point when you should have stopped. The Tao was guiding you, but you overrode its voice."

It was so.

"When you push yourself beyond your point of stress, you will be set back. Now you will have to stay in bed for a day or two to catch up with yourself."

"But I want to help you again tomorrow, master. I do not want to shirk my responsibility."

"Your only responsibility is to stay with the Tao," he told me firmly. "Don't worry about me. You can help me most by getting better. Your happiness is more of a blessing than your pain."

That's not what my parents told me. They said that the more I sacrifice, the more I contribute.

"Get some sleep. I will check on you in the morning." He patted me on the shoulder, pulled the blanket up over my chest, and rose. He blew out the candle and closed the door silently, leaving me to rest.

Those who know when to stop do not find themselves in trouble.

They remain forever safe.

— 44

Putting the Puzzle Together

Everyone has a piece of the puzzle of life, but no one has the whole picture. An ancient parable tells about an elephant that wandered into a village of blind people. Not knowing what an elephant was, the villagers began to examine the huge animal with their hands. One man grabbed the elephant's trunk and declared, "An elephant is like a snake." Another wrapped his arms around the creature's leg and announced, "An elephant is like a tree trunk." Another touched the tail and told, "An elephant is like a rope." All of the blind people were partially correct, but none of them were totally correct. They accurately identified the parts, but none of them identified the whole, which was far greater than any one person could embrace or, from their limited perspective, understand.

So it is with truth. All religions, philosophies, and lifestyles capture a piece of the Big Picture, but none capture all of it. Some arrogantly tout, "My way is *the* way and the *only* way." But humility would recognize that there are many paths to the mountaintop. Religious wars, inquisitions, crusades, and missionary movements all spring from insecurity. "You must believe as I do. If not, you will go to hell, or I will kill you," speaks of deep primal fear. If our world is ever to come to peace, we must grow beyond such immaturity. When we drop into the Tao, we gain security the ego can never garner. Then we release others from the burden of our projection and free them to walk their path.

To put the puzzle together, we must acknowledge the contribution of each philosophy as well as its deficits. Every belief system contains an element of truth and an element of illusion. Purists of each belief spotlight the value of that path, but they also magnify its shortcomings. For example, the hippies were visionaries. They recognized the shallowness and ills of a world suffocating in war, greed, and competition, and perceived there must be a better way to live. So they dropped out, grew organic gardens, smoked pot, and established communes—all of which served in their own way. But the movement did not have the grounding, stamina, or self-discipline to create real, effective, and lasting change. Many adherents were so absorbed in the stratosphere that they didn't get much done on earth. I once hired a hippie-lifestyle fellow to live as a caretaker on my property. One morning I had an appointment for a real estate appraiser to come to my house. Beforehand I had to drop my car off for a repair, and my caretaker agreed to meet me at the repair shop and give me a ride home at 11 A.M. When 11 came and went, I phoned him and, to my surprise, found him still at home. When I asked him why he had not come to pick me up at the agreed time, he answered, "Sorry, man, I don't live in time." Being a longtime meditator, I understood where he was coming from. But I also realized that the world works better when we keep our agreements. I helped him discover the value of time when I gave him some time to find a new job.

On the other side of the yin-yang equation, the corporate world is extremely efficient when it comes to getting things done. Companies achieve success by keeping agreements, meeting deadlines, and manufacturing products that work. But much of the corporate world is heartless and does not hold a vision beyond profits. Many corporate workers come to my seminars burned out from the pressure of overbearing companies that keep piling more jobs on their employees while reducing benefits and acknowledgments. My clients are disheartened by the insatiable greed and lack of integrity they observe. They yearn to work for a more humane employer or set up an entrepreneurial venture that cares for its customers and staff rather than exploiting them.

If I could create a "University of Life in Balance," I would put hippies to work in a corporation for a year, and send corporate executives to a commune in Sedona, Maui, or Sonoma. Both groups would initially have a hard time adjusting, but eventually each would recognize the value of the lifestyle alternative in which they were immersed. Then they could go home and integrate the best of both worlds.

Fortunately, I don't have to create that university. Life has already set it up by making indulgence in extremes self-policing.

When we swing too far to one end of the pendulum, we are forced in the opposite direction. After experiencing both polarities, we extract the best of both worlds and find a middle way that works. A number of former hippies have figured out how to live in time and created companies with integrity and compassion. Whole Foods Market, Ben & Jerry's ice cream, Tom's of Maine, Burt's Bees, and Celestial Seasonings tea, for example, are the progeny of individuals who have merged vision with action and generated consciously created products with widespread positive effects.

Filmmaker Patrick Takaya Solomon interviewed me in his documentary *Finding Joe*, which elucidates the teachings of visionary mythologist Joseph Campbell. During the filming I asked Patrick what had motivated him to produce this movie. "For many years I directed television commercials," he told me. "Then I got tired of selling lies and I decided I would rather sell truth." *Finding Joe* went on to be an award-winning success. Solomon even received a request from President Obama to view the film. This project is a compelling example of a person who gained grounded skills in the corporate world, and then applied them to an uplifting project. Buddha and Lao Tse would call this "right livelihood."

The ten thousand things carry yin and embrace yang.

They achieve harmony by combining these forces.

— 42

Connect the Dots

All good in the world contains the potential to be used for evil and all evil contains the potential to be used for good. Everything holds the seed of its opposite. Have another look at the yin-yang symbol and you will see that within the white section there is a small black dot, and within the black section there is a small white dot.

This illustrates that the ego can exploit good for dark purposes, while higher wisdom can turn apparent curses into blessings.

For example, religions were founded by prophets who had lofty visions and noble intentions to bring healing and uplift-ment to the world. But then people with selfish motives infil-trated religions and twisted the faith to their own foul purposes. While elements of religion remain pure, other elements fall to evil, represented by the dark dot in the light field. Nothing in the world of form is totally good or totally bad. How we use things determines their purpose, value, and results. Take care to not give your power away to a person or group you believe is perfect. Imperfections will surely arise. Welcome to duality.

> *Better stop short than fill to the brim.*
> *Oversharpen the blade, and the edge will soon blunt.*
>
> *——— 9*

On the other side of the spectrum, for every dark experi-ence, something good comes of it. Sickness is an invitation for a course correction to improve the quality of your life. Painful relationships move you to honor yourself and claim better. Los-ing a job can motivate you to create a more meaningful, pas-sion-filled career. Overbearing monarchs incite downtrodden people to establish democracies. The crucified and resurrected

Christ taught that he—like all of us—is greater than the body. Like the white dot within the black space, the spiritual master finds light in the midst of the darkness. If you feel engulfed in darkness, look for the light. It is there. Our true power lies in the vision we use to see the world and what we make of things rather than what they make of us.

How to Make the Middle Path Work for You

Some people take radical leaps of faith and create dramatic positive changes for themselves and the world. Yet most people do better to walk the middle path. I mentioned my clients who wish to leave their corporate jobs and create careers more aligned with their values. Many such individuals struggle with whether or not to quit their job and dive into an impassioned alternative career. Meanwhile they fear they will not have the income to support themselves and their families. I usually tell such clients that there may be a middle path that can satisfy both sides of the equation. "How about keeping your day job while you simultaneously develop your entrepreneurial venture?" I ask them. "Then you can maintain an income while fulfilling your creative promptings. At some point you may develop your exciting project to the point that it will support you. Then you can leave your job without fear or stress." Clients usually really like this formula and choose that course, which would make Lao Tse smile.

Masters of the Tao keep their head in the clouds and their feet on the ground. Take a moment now to consider if you have gone to an extreme in any element of your life. Do you eat too much junk food, or are you a health food fanatic? Do you rest enough to offset your work? Are you so intent on keeping your house clean that you get upset at the kids or the dog for bringing dirt in? Do you believe your religion is the only way, or do you have space for others to find their own path to God? Are you stuck on your party's political beliefs, or is it possible the other party may be right at least some of the time? Are you so vehemently against anything that you cannot see the reason it exists?

Those who stand on tiptoe are not steady.
Those who stride cannot maintain the pace.
— 24

Now consider how you might be empowered by choosing more of a middle path and allowing what you don't understand or agree with to have its place. What a relief that things don't always have to be a certain way! Hallelujah! You are free! Chinese medicine seeks to balance the patient. If too hot, make colder. If too damp, make drier. If too fast, make slower. Every experience moves you to achieve greater balance in your life. The Tao within you is telling you exactly what you need to do, but you must be willing to heed the signs.

Knowing harmony is constancy.
Knowing constancy is enlightenment.
— 55

The Ultimate Balancing Act

Paradox delivers the ultimate teaching of balance: two ideas that appear to be contradictory are simultaneously true. Herein lies your point of power. If you can accept the reality of two apparent opposites, you are at altitude on the mountain of mastery. The thinking mind goes haywire when it attempts to integrate polarities. But your inner sage can sit with apparent contradiction. Don't fight it. Just enjoy it and let your oppressive left-brain intellect short-circuit as you shift to the exhilaration of right-brain mysticism.

The truth often sounds paradoxical.

— 78

Seek perfection but allow for imperfection. Let what appears to not be working be a part of what is working. Let night and day make each other more poignant. Let evil give way to good. Allow what seems apart to come together. Life is not a question of balance. Balance is the answer to the questions of life.

Moderation is the silken string running through the pearl-chain of all virtues.

— THOMAS FULLER

IN THE ZONE

The space between heaven and earth is like a
bellows . . . The more it moves, the more it yields.

—— 5

More than anything else, high school sophomore Jason McElwain wanted to play basketball. But being autistic and only five feet, six inches in height, there was no way he was going to make the basketball team. Coach Jim Johnson kindly dubbed Jason the team manager, gave him jobs to help the team, and let him sit on the bench during the games.

Two years later, when the final varsity game of the season came, signaling the end of Jason's high school sports career, Coach Johnson decided to give the kid a parting moment he would remember. With less than four minutes left in the last quarter, he sent Jason onto the court. What happened next was nothing less than a miracle. During that very short time, Jason scored 20 points, including six three pointers from *way* out. The crowd of spectators, well aware of Jason's "limitations" and history, went wild. By the time the final buzzer sounded, the "little kid who couldn't" was a hero. (Watch it all on YouTube, "J Mac—A Hoop Dream.")

When word got out about this unbelievable feat, Jason attained national notoriety. His family received 25 calls from movie producers seeking to dramatize his performance; the President of the United States made a trip to Jason's hometown to congratulate him; and he appeared on national television shows. Two years later Jason authored *The Game of My Life*. All a result of less than four astounding minutes. Coach Johnson later stated, "He was unstoppable."

Was Jason McElwain's superhuman performance a quirk of nature, or is there a scientific principle behind his feat? Did the young man achieve some rare state of consciousness that enabled him to do the impossible? And if so, is that state available to you and me?

Lao Tse assures us that the Tao can and will enable you to do what needs to be done, from the ordinary to the extraordinary. When you partner with a power that *transcends* the world, you have dominion *over* the world. With the Tao behind you, miracles will unfold before your eyes.

When I arrived at Lao Tse's cabin he was nowhere to be found. The place was silent except for some chickens clucking in the yard. I feared that the master had gone away and I had missed him. I searched the cabin, to no avail.

I walked around to the backyard where there was a small shed. Lao Tse hardly went in there except to get gardening tools. As I approached, I heard a rhythmic squeaking sound. Curious, I walked to a paper window on the side of the shed, pulled it aside, and peered in.

There I saw Lao Tse seated at a pottery wheel, throwing a pot. I had seen the wheel in the shed, buried under other tools, but this was the first time I saw him using it. As his foot pumped the wheel, his wet hands were fashioning a *dou*, a wide-mouthed urn that people in the earlier Shang dynasty used to make offerings to various gods. During our Zhou dynasty, people no longer offer them to gods, but instead place them in their homes as symbols of opulence. Knowing Lao Tse as I did, he surely was not making the *dou* as an offering to the gods or as a personal trophy. It was simply a popular art form he would make as a gift.

Positioned far enough behind the master that he did not know I was watching, I was captivated to watch his hands dance over the wet clay. His touch was firm but graceful. As the wheel turned in a musical cadence, his arms and head moved with the rhythm, his body emanating the delight of a child. Simply watching him was a teaching in joy.

Then something astonishing happened that I don't even know if I can describe in words. I'll just say it: Lao Tse disappeared. One moment I saw him leaning over the wheel, and the next moment all I could see was the wheel turning with the *dou* rotating atop it. I blinked to be sure I was not imagining this, but after a few moments the master was still not there. I lifted up the paper window to get a fuller view, in case this was a trick of light or perspective—but he was still gone. The wheel and the pot were turning by themselves. I was shocked. What had become of the man at the wheel? I forced myself to take some deep breaths to keep me grounded in the face of this weird vision. I began to fear that he had traveled to some other dimension and he was gone forever.

Then he was there again. I can't say how long he was gone—it was at least a few minutes. When I saw him I was so relieved. Still stunned, I stepped away and sat down with my back against the trunk of a tree, trying to ground myself.

After a while Lao Tse emerged from the shed and greeted me. I wondered if I should tell him what I had seen and ask him how he had disappeared. But I decided to just leave the experience at that. It was a glorious intimate moment in the master's world and I did not want him to know I was spying on him.

A few months later Lao Tse and I went to an art exhibit by a famous painter. There he told me that true artists merge with the Tao and disappear into their work. The artist and the art become one. The small self becomes a vessel for the Grand Self and is indistinguishable from the Source. That was the answer I was looking for. I will never forget the moment when I saw Lao Tse disappear into the Tao.

Shape the clay into a vessel;
It is the space within that makes it useful.
Cut doors and windows for a room;
It is the holes that make it useful.
Therefore profit comes from what is there;
Usefulness from what is not there.

—— 11

The Zone Te Ching

We all disappear into the Tao from time to time. Surely you have had the experience of becoming so absorbed in an activity you love that you forget all else and you become one with what you are doing. Time loosens its grip and you dwell in the timeless moment. When I write, for example, two or three hours pass that seem like 15 minutes. I step back, look at the computer, and I see a chapter that wasn't there before. My sense of "I" disappeared, the Tao took over, and created through me. Many artists, musicians, and inventors report that their most important works are born when their small self dissolves into a broader self that achieves a remarkable result.

While the Tao has been described in many ways throughout the ages, one most recently popularized is "the Zone." An entire field called "Zone psychology" has developed. The Zone is a state of consciousness that transcends the normal and enables us to achieve extraordinary results. Think of the Zone as a room in the universe where everything functions at its highest potential. This room is filled with such ease, grace, and flow that everything within it works perfectly. Jesus said, "In my Father's house there are many mansions," indicating there are an infinite number of parallel realities, each of which seems real when you are in it. Spiritual mastery consists of consciously choosing the room you dwell in and using it to your benefit and that of others. Every human being has the capacity to enter the Zone and benefit from its gifts, and everyone does, at some time. Ernest Holmes, founder of Science of Mind, stated, "There is room at the top for everyone."

Less and less is done

Until non-action is achieved.

When nothing is done, nothing is left undone.

— 48

How to Get in the Zone

"If the Zone is available to everyone, how can I get into it so I can reap its rewards?" you ask.

The answer may surprise you: *Lighten up and do what makes you happy.*

That's it. The dynamic is simple, but requires understanding and practice. Here's how it works:

Just as you need a key card containing a configured magnetic strip to open the door of a hotel room, to enter the Zone your mental and emotional state must match it. That configuration is never based on the dense frequencies of struggle, pain, sacrifice, resistance, or complaint. It is always based on the higher frequencies of joy, trust, flow, and positive vision. If you are angry, upset, or defiant, you can't get there from here. You need to elevate your consciousness. You can't get to something you love by doing something you hate. You can't get to ease by way of struggle; to peace by way of conflict; to wholeness by way of sacrifice; or to self-affirmation by way of self-denial. You have to attain a state of being that is closer to the experience you desire. You don't have to become a total master of happiness overnight, but you do have to step at least a little bit in that direction. *A Course in Miracles* tells us that all that is required for a miracle is "a little willingness." When you do anything that makes you happy, you maximize the Zone's ability to find you.

Take a moment now to consider what brings you the most joy in your life. Perhaps it's dancing; playing music; creating works of art; gardening; connecting with your children or grandchildren; playing with your pet; traveling; or some odd activity that most other people would not choose or understand, but that genuinely makes you happy. If it brings you joy, that's reason enough to do it. You don't need to justify or explain your delight to anyone. Well-being is self-affirming.

Coaching clients often ask me, "How can I find my ultimate passionate path and know my purpose in life?" I reply, "Tell me two or three things you do that you most enjoy." The client answers, for example, "I love to play my guitar, write in my journal, and walk by the sea." Then I tell the client in a serious voice, "I am now receiving a message directly from God. The Lord is telling me exactly what you need to do to live your purpose and be happy. Are you ready to hear your answer?"

"Yes! Yes!" the client replies excitedly.

"Do you have something to write with?"

"Yes, right here. Please, please tell me."

For dramatic effect, I continue to tease the client for a while. Finally, when he or she can wait no longer, I say, "To find your true passion and purpose in life, the Creator wants you to play your guitar, write in your journal, and walk by the sea."

While I milk the process for fun, the message is serious. Your purpose in life is intrinsically connected to your passion, and your passion is present right where you stand. While you might argue, "I have no passion," or "I don't know what my passion is," you *do* have passion—if you didn't, you wouldn't be alive. While part of you may have lost touch with your passion, another part knows precisely where it lives. Ask the part of you that knows your path and purpose to reveal itself, and it will. If you try to grasp the Big Picture of your entire life's purpose, you will get muddled and confused. If you demand to know it all now, you will become even more overwhelmed. But if you start by acting on the passion that already exists, even if it is the tiniest of trickles, it will expand to a stream and then a mighty river. I have guided thousands of people through this process, and nearly every one of them has found at least a thread of their passionate purpose. Following that thread will lead you home.

When you do what you love, the grace of God reaches down to meet your upstretched hand. Of course you also have to develop and practice the skills to perfect the form of your expression. But discipline is not the enemy of joy; when employed in the service of a gratifying goal, it becomes "blis-sipline." Take whatever steps you can to achieve what you desire, and let the Tao fill in any remaining blanks. Never try to force the Zone. You couldn't if you tried. Trying is the opposite of allowing. Stepping into the Zone is the result of intention, action, timing, chemistry, flow, and surrender. Just do your part and the universe will do its part.

> *Giving birth and nourishing,*
>
> *Bearing yet not possessing,*
>
> *Working yet not taking credit,*
>
> *Leading yet not dominating,*
>
> *This is the Primal Virtue.*
>
> — 10

The Other Door

The other door to the Zone is marked, "Quit Doing What Grates Against You." When you do something you would not choose, or resist something you must do, you distance yourself from the Zone and you make it hard for it to find you. To reclaim the Tao, find a way to either release the disdained activity or make peace with it. Every act you do either brings you greater life or deadens you. You can't be partially pregnant. Either you are or you aren't. Either you are headed toward greater aliveness or toward oblivion.

Take a sheet of paper now and draw a vertical line down the center. Title the left column, "What Brings Me Life." Title the right column, "What Deadens Me." Then list every activity you engage in, small or large, that matches either of these themes. *Only total honesty will work here.* When you complete both lists, you are looking at your up-close-and-personal map of how to get into the Zone. Here's *Tao Te Ching* in 10 words:

Do what brings you life. Quit doing what deadens you.

If you follow this path with sincere intention, you will accelerate your journey at light speed. Every worthy religion, spiritual path, and philosophy boils down to this. Now it's up to you to do it.

> *Don't ask yourself what the world needs; ask yourself what*
> *makes you come alive. And then go and do that. Because*
> *what the world needs is people who have come alive.*
>
> — HOWARD THURMAN

The Meeting Place

When you are in the Zone, you stand at the meeting place of heaven and earth. Despite all the stories you have been told to the contrary, utter well-being is where life wants you to live. *A Course in Miracles* asks us to remember, "God's will for me is perfect happiness." Your divinely appointed place in the world, fulfilling relationships, and brimming abundance are seeking you at this very moment. But you must let them in. While you are searching for the Zone, it is searching for you. When you allow it, miracles happen. Then, like Jason McElwain, the little kid who couldn't, but did, *you* will become unstoppable.

> *Those who follow the Tao*
> *Are at one with the Tao. . . .*
> *When you are at one with the Tao,*
> *the Tao welcomes you.*
>
> — 23

LIFE AFTER ISM

The Tao is forever undefined.
Small though it is in the unformed state,
it cannot be grasped.
If leaders could harness it,
The ten thousand things would naturally obey.
Heaven and earth would come together
And gentle rain fall.
People would no longer need laws and all
things would take their course.

—— 32

Lao Tse was the original out-of-the-box thinker. He knew a reality so vast that no concept could capture it. While we can all access that limitless expanse, we tend to live in the cubicles our minds fabricate, none of which contain the whole truth. A Zen master advised, "Do not mistake the finger pointing at the moon for the moon itself." Words, philosophies, and religions are at best fingers pointing at the moon. They lead to something the intellect cannot embrace. If you worship a finger, the universe will give you the finger. Lao Tse would have us look beyond and bask in the glow of the moon.

The master opens the door to the unspeakable infinite in the very first lines of *Tao Te Ching*:

The Tao that can be told is not the eternal Tao.

The name that can be named is not the eternal name.

— 1

Yet we go to great lengths to name the Tao by "isms," "ians," and "ish's" that form the containers we hope will grasp what cannot be contained. All such rooms of mind serve their purpose, but they ultimately imprison. The eminent psychotherapist Carl Jung declared, "Thank God I am not a Jungian." Likewise, Lao Tse would not call himself a Taoist. Noble and helpful as the religious tradition is, the old master could not live inside a case. Even while Lao Tse warned against efforts to organize truth, an "ism" has grown up around his teachings. If I had to join a religious movement, Taoism would be a worthy prospect. But I would not find Lao Tse at its meetings. He would be home writing,

Look, it cannot be seen—it is beyond form.

Listen, it cannot be heard—it is beyond sound.

Grasp, it cannot be held—it is intangible.

These three are indefinable;

Therefore they are joined in one.

— 14

Love It, Don't Label It

The ego, in its fundamental insecurity, believes it can gain control over an uncontrollable universe by manufacturing endless boxes it can stack neatly to assuage its sense of powerlessness. When people meet my dogs in public, for example, they usually ask the same questions: "What kind are they?" "How old are they?" and "Where did you get them?" Likewise, we pigeonhole people. When describing someone, you might say, "Noriko is a slender, attractive Asian woman with long hair, about thirty-five." In that one short sentence we reduce a living spirit to no less than seven compartments: name, body type, looks, race, gender, hairstyle, and age. No wonder we feel lonely, vulnerable, and less-than. Nearly every way we think about ourselves and others is based on difference, rating, and judgment! Mark Twain said, "Comparison is the death of joy."

We most typically shrink our infinite selves to bodies only. If you search Match.com for a date, the first search criterion is "appearance." Potential dates must make the physical cut before we even consider personality. Body first, spirit second (if at all). The consequence of constant identification with the body and limiting labels is depression, for such a way of seeing overlooks the reality and magnitude of our spirit. It is no wonder, then, that nearly 35 million Americans regularly take prescription antidepressants, and a far greater number self-medicate with alcohol, recreational drugs, and mind-numbing soft addictions like television, Internet, video games, and smartphones. Limiting ourselves to our bodies reduces us to the only part of us that will die, which leaves us fearing death and seeking life in aberrant ways.

The good news is that there is another part of us that extends far beyond our ascribed boundaries, the one Lao Tse would have us know:

> *Stand before it and there is no beginning.*
>
> *Follow it and there is no end.*
>
> *Stay with the ancient Tao,*
>
> *Move with the present.*
>
> *— 14*

The spiritual journey takes us from form to formlessness; from body to spirit; from limits to freedom. This is the path every human being must eventually walk. Ultimately all rivers flow to the ocean and we all reemerge into the Tao. When we stretch beyond labels, we hasten our homecoming.

One day a family of gorgeous little yellow birds found its way to our lawn. I asked Dee, "Shall we look them up on the Web to see what kind they are?"

"Let's not," she replied. "I don't want to give them a name. I just want to enjoy them as they are."

How refreshing! Wouldn't it be wonderful if we could likewise set ourselves and the people we know free of stifling genres? We don't see each other as we are. We see each other through highly filtered lenses. If we recognized our true nature, we would see only brilliant light. All else is the result of massive layering. The intellect is obsessed with dissecting life into smaller and smaller pieces. It is said, "An expert is someone who knows more and more about less and less until he knows everything about nothing." A spiritual master, by contrast, knows less and less about more and more until he knows everything as it truly is.

> *Once the whole is divided, the parts need names.*
>
> *There are already enough names.*
>
> *We need to know when to stop.*
>
> *— 32*

Stars and Lilies

The universe was created in utter perfection and does not need our help to improve it. Humanity's attempts to override nature have separated us from our source and destroyed what can save us. A camera can point to the glory of a pristine forest, but cannot create it. No smartphone is smart enough to spin a planet into orbit. God speaks to us daily, but we rarely take the time to listen. Nature is my church. When I walk in nature I know the Tao. No building, altar, or ritual is necessary. Human beings have created magnificent, awe-inspiring cathedrals, but none can surpass the wonder of a starry night.

Ralph Waldo Emerson said it this way:

If the stars should appear one night in a thousand years,
how would men believe and adore; and preserve
for many generations the remembrance of the city of God
which had been shown! But every night come out
these envoys of beauty, and light the universe
with their admonishing smile.

Jesus offered the same teaching in the language of his time:

Consider the lilies of the field, how they grow.
They do not toil and neither do they spin
and yet I say to you that even Solomon in all his glory
was not arrayed like one of these.

Jesus and Lao Tse would have gotten along famously. They both recognized the Source of beauty and blessing, in us and all around us.

Ever desireless, one can see the mystery.

Ever desiring, one can see the manifestations.

These two spring from the same source
but differ in name . . .

The gate to all mystery.

—— 1

Life beyond Belief

All beliefs are temporary and ultimately evolve to something different. There will come a time when everything you now believe will not be true for you. As much as you are sure you know how it is, one day you will change your mind about how it is. Never argue that your way is the only way or the right way. One day you will be proven wrong, even to yourself. That day will be joyful because you will leave a smaller room to enter a greater one. Many years ago I adopted a vegetarian diet. I believe that eating low on the food chain is healthy, ethical, and contributes to the well-being of the planet. I was also taught that a plant-based diet renders one more peaceful. Then I saw a documentary that caused me to revisit those assumptions. *Guided by the Stars: The Stargate of Samburu* chronicles the adventures of Rhodia Mann, a British woman who has periodically lived with the Samburu tribe in Africa. The Samburu diet, she explains, consists of meat, blood, and milk—a vegetarian's nightmare! Yet the Samburu are extremely healthy, slim, and agile. In the film we meet herbalist healer Lesha Lang, who appears to be 40-ish, but is actually 70 years of age! The Samburu are an extremely peaceful and spiritual culture. While the tribes in the surrounding region are aggressive and warlike, the pacifistic Samburu do not engage in conflict with them.

That information pulled the rug out from under my belief that in order to be healthy, youthful, slim, and peaceful, you must leave the cows in the field and keep them off the dining room table. I also know people fervently dedicated to a pure vegetarian diet who have gotten sick and died at young ages, and others who are cranky and dogmatic. So, much as I would like to take refuge in my belief system, it appears that there is no absolute, across-the-board relationship between diet, health, and attitude. I continue to maintain a light diet because I feel better with it and I believe in its ethical and environmental value. But now I have space for others to choose a different diet and have it work for them. More human suffering springs from narrow-mindedness and aggressive imposition of beliefs than from diet. Jesus said, "It is not what goes in a person's mouth that defiles him, but what comes out of it." The need to be right is what makes things go wrong. If insecure religions, political parties, cultures, teachers, spouses, and parents would just quit trying to force others to adopt their beliefs, violence would abate, humanity would grow beyond its dogmatic immaturity, and society would evolve rapidly.

If those in power observed this,
The ten thousand things would develop naturally.
— 37

While passing through a village on my way to visit the master, I came upon a crowd gathered in the central square. I worked my way through the group to find a man lying on the ground, bleeding from the stomach. A woman kneeled at his side, dabbing a cloth at the wound. An old man rolled up his jacket and formed a pillow for the injured man to rest his head. He looked pale and quite weak. I wondered if he might die.

"What happened?" I asked a fellow standing next to me.

"This man came through town looking for some work. Zheng Guo hired him to pick some crops, and promised him a portion of what he harvested as his pay. After the day's work, Zheng Guo asked him to make an offering of a part of his earnings to Hou-ji, Zheng Guo's family deity. When this man told Zheng Guo that he did not believe in that god and would not make an offering, the two got into an argument. The conflict heated until Zheng Guo pulled out a knife and stabbed the man. He told him, 'Anyone who will not humble himself before Hou-ji deserves to die.'"

Shaken, I took my leave and hastened to Lao Tse's cabin. I told him about the incident and asked him why a man would stab someone over an offering to a god.

"People feel powerless and insecure," he answered. "So they place their faith in external gods, rituals, and objects they believe will save them. Then they demand others must agree with them so they can feel validated. When they cannot control nonbelievers, they need to get rid of them."

"What a sick way of thinking!"

"It is," the master agreed. "But humanity has fallen prey to many beliefs that keep people living small. Only when we remember the vastness of the Tao and its all-embracing nature do we return to our right mind and restore harmony to the world. Then we do not need other people to agree with us in order for us to feel justified."

> The master's words made sense. "Does that mean we should do away with religion, tradition, and rituals?"
>
> "No, those institutions serve when practiced with pure intent. When religions unite people, they are an expression of the Tao. When people use them as an excuse to hurt each other, they lose the Great Way. My religion is kindness. When we help each other, even in the smallest way, we fulfill the purpose of all religions."
>
> The master set a bowl of rice and vegetables and a cup of tea before me. "Have something to eat. You've had a hard day. Don't add to the conflict you have seen by carrying your disturbance. When your heart is at peace, you are worshipping as creation intended."

I believe that the only true religion consists of having a good heart.

— His Holiness the Dalai Lama

Who Is Closer?

The Tao does not separate, but enfolds. Any form of divisiveness only reinforces the illusions that keep humanity in pain. After I heard about a fundamentalist Christian group that announced a massive Koran-burning, I asked my teacher why people are so attracted to narrow-minded fundamentalist groups. She answered, "They don't have to think for themselves and they get to feel that they are right."

By contrast, consider the incident in Pakistan in which an extremist Muslim faction murdered at least 80 worshippers as they exited All Saints Church in Peshawar. The next week a group of 250 people of all faiths, mostly Muslims, surrounded the church, held hands, and formed a human chain to protect Christians as they departed. Which group, the Christians who sought to burn the Koran, or the Muslims who protected the Christians, were living in harmony with the Tao? The answer is obvious. It is unlikely that the Muslim protectors had studied *Tao Te Ching*. They were just living it. There are also Christians who respect other spiritual paths and seek to connect rather than separate. They are the true disciples of Christ.

If you need to be right by making others wrong, you will not find a home in the Tao. *A Course in Miracles* asks, "Would you prefer that you be right or happy?" If you get bogged down in self-righteousness, you will become sidetracked from the Great Way and not receive the gifts it offers.

> *Never believe anything that requires you to hate people*
> *who do not believe it.*
>
> — ROBERT BRAULT

When you follow the Tao, you are always right, because the Tao knows what to do in every situation, and it will guide you impeccably. Next week or next year, today's course of action may be totally inappropriate. Gandhi said, "I am committed to truth, not consistency." The Tao is not attractive to people who need a rigid belief system for them to feel secure. Those who trust that the formless is the master of form find a home in spaciousness.

> *Passersby may stop for music and good food,*
> *But it is not possible to describe the Tao.*
> *Without substance or flavor,*
> *It cannot be seen, it cannot be heard,*
> *And yet it cannot be exhausted.*
>
> —— 35

The Shelf Life of Institutions

We are living at a time when many of the institutions we have long held dear have either outlived their purpose or have become so corrupted that they are causing more harm than service. Significant elements of government, politics, the economy, education, health care, religion, and the media have become dysfunctional. Many relationships and marriages are based more on illusions than truth. Within all of these institutions there are dedicated individuals who live true to the original vision, but these represent the minority. When organizations become top-heavy, they crumble, gradually or suddenly, and newer, more purposeful forms in harmony with the Tao take their place. The universe is eternally self-correcting, advancing to higher levels of expression. Classic Hindu philosophy tells us that we are living in the time of the Kali Yuga, when humanity has drifted into the darkness as far from the Creator's intention as it can possibly go. When we recognize that there is no other way to head but toward the light and we are moved to reclaim our spiritual destiny, that is what will happen. There are signs that this is occurring now, individually and collectively. Meanwhile, elements of the darkness are being magnified to an insane degree. Such intensification must occur to make the nightmare so obvious that we have no choice but to wake up. Such evolution is uncomfortable, but necessary.

To live true to the Tao, look clearly at your organizational affiliations and ask if the organization and your participation in it reflect the Tao or if the institution has veered from the purpose for which it was created. What would it take to bring your life into greater alignment with the Tao, within the institution or without it? Such an inquiry, while initially challenging, can be extremely liberating. The only thing worse than discovering that you have been participating in a dysfunctional system is to stay in it. Acknowledging that something is not working is the first step to making it work. Behold the adventure set before you. Shrink not from reality. It is calling you to claim it.

The greatest Virtue is to follow Tao
and Tao alone.

— 21

Where Does Your Faith Live?

Everyone has faith in something. What you have faith in determines the results you get. If you have faith in boxes, you will live in a box. If you have faith in what is unlimited, you will live free. All "isms" serve, but at some point the master of the Tao must grow beyond them. She must honor and use the 10,000 things, but not be enslaved by them. You cannot bottle truth, own it, copyright it, brand it, sell it, scare people into believing it, beat nonbelievers over the head with it, or claim that yours is the only truth and no one else has it. The moment you say, "This alone is true," you leave something else out. This is why the Tao ultimately leads to silence, where riches beyond words are found. The ego urges us to avoid silence because it is empty. The spirit urges us to dive into silence because it is full.

Blind faith leaves people sightless. The Tao calls us to never swallow any belief system whole, but to be discerning about what is true and what is illusion laid over truth in truth's name.

Every decision we make is between littleness and magnitude. Only a courageous few are willing to peer over the horizon. You are invited to live among them.

I would rather have a mind opened by
wonder than one closed by belief.

— GARY SPENCE

THE FINAL
FRONTIER

Thirty spokes converge upon a single hub;
it is on the hole in the center that
the use of the cart hinges.

—— 11

When science-fiction prophet Gene Roddenberry penned his classic introduction to the *Star Trek* television series, he had no idea how his words would bring the Tao to life in the 20th century and beyond. *"Space—the final frontier"* points us to a far vaster realm than the expanse rocket ships must pierce. It describes the inner domain each of us must conquer if we are to find the peace we seek.

You may not realize how much your psychic space has been compromised. How many scattered thoughts rampage through your mind in the course of a day? How many texts, e-mails, and websites do you click on? How many tasks sit on your to-do list? How many advertising impressions impinge on your awareness? How many people do you see on the subway, or cars do you pass on the highway? How many television channels do you surf? How many pieces of sensational news flash at you in one newscast? Is it any surprise that so many people suffer from attention deficit disorder and stress-related maladies? When we are overwhelmed with data, we can't think straight, feel relaxed, or make decisions in harmony with the Tao. Lao Tse left a city

2,500 years ago to get away from a distracted society. What would he say about the world today?

Even then the master was aware of the battle between intention and distraction for ownership of your soul. He urged us to found ourselves in inner quietude rather than allowing external noise to displace it.

One afternoon while I was working in Lao Tse's yard, a young woman burst through the gate. She ran to the front door, pounded on it, and called in tears, "Master! I must speak with you."

Lao Tse soon appeared at the door and stepped outside. "What is the matter, my dear?" he asked with his unique blend of full presence and quiet detachment.

"My parents want me to marry a man I can't stand. He is older and boorish and domineering. I would rather kill myself than marry him!"

Lao Tse did not respond immediately with advice. Instead, he invited the young lady to sit next to him on a wooden bench beside his door. She seemed relieved to have the master's attention. I did not want to invade their privacy, so I moved to prune a tree several yards away, but I could still hear the conversation.

The woman went on about her parents, this man, and other upsets in her life. Lao Tse did not make any comments. He simply nodded occasionally in sympathy.

As I moved on with my work about the yard, I could barely hear their words, but I sensed the change in the woman's tone of voice. As time went on, she became much calmer. Her tension dissipated and a small smile grew over her lips. Finally she stood and I heard her say, "Thank you so much, Master Lao Tse. You were the perfect person for me to talk to. Now I know exactly what to do." The young lady bowed, turned, and exited the yard an entirely different person than the one who had entered in a frenzy just a short time earlier.

I approached the master. "What a change!" I told him. "You must have given her excellent advice."

He smiled a knowing, almost sneaky smile. "Not at all."

"You didn't tell her what to do? She seemed so much more confident after your conversation."

"It wasn't much of a conversation," he replied. "She did most of the talking."

I was confused. "Then what did you do that helped her so much?"

"I just gave her space. She was upset and she needed to vent. She considered me to be a safe person, so she poured out her heart. When she felt free to express herself, she arrived at her own conclusion. Her problem was not her fiancé. Her problem was that she felt unseen and unheard. When I considered her important enough to give her my full attention, she felt relieved and saw clearly what to do."

I had a hard time believing that Lao Tse could have helped someone so much without saying hardly a word. I must have looked pretty dumbfounded.

"Come with me," said the master, motioning for me to join him inside his cabin. He walked to a corner, reached into a wooden box, and picked up a few rolled parchments. Then he took a calligraphy brush and a small vial of ink. He spread a blank parchment out on a table and slowly wrote out the character for "space." Then he wrote "space" again. And again. And again. He must have written the word 50 times until the entire parchment was filled with the word *space*.

"What do you see?" Lao Tse asked me.

"Space?"

"Look again."

I kept studying the parchment. I couldn't think of another answer.

"You are not seeing space. You are seeing a parchment filled with the word *space*. But the word is not the same as the experience of space. Really, how much space is there on the page?"

I studied the page again. "Hardly any."

The master took a second blank parchment and unrolled it on the table. In the center of the page he wrote the character for "thing." "Now what do you see?"

"A thing?"

"Look again."

I stepped back and realized that the parchment was largely empty. "I see lots of space on the page."

He smiled as if to acknowledge that I was finally getting somewhere.

"And how clear is the 'thing'?"

"Very clear. Much clearer than the first parchment where the words for *space* filled the page to the point of being muddled."

"The purpose of space is to contrast with things," my teacher explained. "When you have a balance of space and things, things become clear and so does the space."

He reached to the first parchment and spread it out side by side with the second one. "Which parchment brings you greater peace when you look at it?"

There was no question about it. The first parchment was cluttered and ugly. The second one breathed. "This one, for sure," I told him.

"Give yourself space to be what you are. Give others space to be what they are. Then everything will make itself clear."

Lao Tse rolled up the parchments and placed them back in a box on the floor. Then he stepped away, giving me space to absorb the lesson.

Empty yourself of everything.

Let the mind become still.

—— 16

The Fear to Look Within

Our obsession with doing is not imposed upon us by some outside source. It is a choice. Ceaseless activity is contrived by the ego to keep us from facing ourselves. Inescapable as our constant running seems, we prefer it because we fear to look within. We believe that if we faced ourselves, we would find pain and darkness so overwhelming that we would rush to die at our own hand. So we create an endless stream of errands, tasks, obligations, problems, dramas, and emergencies to keep us preoccupied with the outer world.

James Thurber advised, "All men should strive to learn before they die, what they are running from and to, and why."

It is a rare and courageous person who is willing to lay aside the quest for outer-world achievement and instead dive within for the pearl of great price. Yet eventually, after roaming the earth for lifetimes and going through countless trials and errors, we recognize that external things will not fulfill us. The treasure we seek is soul contentment. When we have that, the external world becomes an afterthought.

When we take space to be with ourselves, the problems that appeared so real and overwhelming lose their power over us. They *seemed* to have power only because we gave them our attention and belief that they are bigger than we are. We used them as an excuse to bully ourselves. But your true self runs far deeper than anything that happens to you. Jesus said, "He that is in me is greater than he that is in the world." Lao Tse would say, "The Tao lives in the ten thousand things and far beyond them." When we withdraw from our immersion in doingness, we gain perspective, and our worldly affairs assume their proper place in the service of spirit. This is why all great spiritual masters have taken time to retreat. Lao Tse left the city, literally and metaphorically, to reclaim his soul, and he would urge us to take the same journey.

If you do not take care of your soul, the tide of karmic events will force you to do so. You will land in bed or the hospital, or have a nervous breakdown, business failure, divorce, or some other "in-your-face" experience that requires you to address and heal your pain at its root. In that sense, such breakdowns are a blessing. If the breakdown leads to a breakthrough, it has served well. Such upheavals are the Tao announcing loud and clear, "What you have been doing has separated you from yourself, your loved ones, and your life. Please receive this message so you can make a needed course correction and return to what really matters." When you finally listen to the Tao, you will fall on your knees in humble gratitude that the universe was compassionate enough to *not* allow you to continue hurtling over a cliff into oblivion.

The Tao is empty but inexhaustible, bottomless,
the ancestor of it all.
Within it, the sharp edges become smooth;
the twisted knots loosen;
the sun is softened by a cloud;
the dust settles into place . . .

— 4

From Doing to Being

You may believe that if you can just do enough, you will succeed. But *doing* is not effective when it eclipses *being*. If you lose yourself in doing, what you do will bear no fruit. If you can maintain your being, even while doing, you have mastered the formula for living.

Others err in the direction of being without doing. They fantasize and contemplate their goals, but take no action to manifest them. Then they wonder why they have not succeeded. They need to pray with their feet moving.

You are most effective and happiest when you integrate being and doing. The Zen maxim tells us, "Before enlightenment, chop wood and carry water. After enlightenment, chop wood and carry water." When you flow with the Tao, you do not stop doing. You may keep going to your job, texting with friends, going to the gym, and looking for the best deals on Amazon.com. *What* you do may not change that much. *How* you do it changes dramatically. Your life ceases to be a frantic race to nowhere or a frustrating task of pushing a rock up a hill only to have it roll back down on you. Instead, your journey becomes an inspired creative expression. Challenges may show up, but they do not crush you. Instead, you seek to understand how this situation fits into the greater picture of your awakening, and you work the experience in your favor. Thus even difficult encounters become your friends, elements of the broader Tao.

Or, your life may change dramatically as a result of your wake-up call. You may be motivated, as Dag Hammarskjöld visioned, "To be free, to be able to stand up and leave everything behind—without looking back. To say *Yes*—." Some people, upon recognizing that they have gotten painfully disconnected from Source, decide to leave their old life in the dust and they radically reinvent themselves. In the thought-provoking documentary *Minimalism*, we meet a fellow who was offered a junior partnership in a huge financial firm—the promotion he had always dreamed of. But "I walked back into my office and I started weeping because I realized I was completely and utterly trapped and any dream I had of living a life of purpose and meaning . . . and of deliberate intention—those were gone. . . . I took the elevator down 28 stories and that was it. Ever since then I decided that this life was going to be mine and it would be wildly, flamboyantly my life."

As another alternative, you might step off the treadmill and retreat for a while to get your head on straight. Then you return to your activity with your connection renewed and your purpose clarified. This is why I and other teachers offer retreats at which individuals can step away from oppressive routines for a week to renew, refresh, revitalize, regroup, and restore, and then reenter daily life at a higher octave. Jesus went into the desert for 40 days, during which he conquered temptation. Moses scaled Mount Sinai and later descended with the Word of God. Muhammad's first revelation came when he was meditating in a cave on a mountain and was visited by the archangel Gabriel. Then all of these masters returned to the world and delivered the insights they gained.

You need not be a religious prophet to benefit from a retreat. Nor do you need to wait until you can get away for a weekend or week. Do it daily. Set up some kind of meditation, prayer, or soul-renewing activity each day. Begin your day with connection to Source and then take space during your day whenever you can, even for a few moments, to energize your spirit. Then, before you go to bed, devote some time to cleanse your thoughts and emotions and prepare you for deep, healing sleep.

Such moments of claiming space will keep you aligned with the Tao, empower you to move through your activities consciously, and pay off many times over in productivity, prosperity, health, and inner peace.

Ultimately you don't need to go anywhere to find your space. You carry your space with you. Going to a physical space symbolizes going to a spiritual space. As the credit card commercial suggests, "Don't leave home without it." All journeys outward ultimately lead inward, where real answers live. The fool searches in the outer world. The master goes within.

Who can wait quietly while the mud settles?
Who can remain still until the moment of action?

— 15

Stop talking, stop thinking, and there is nothing you will not understand.
Return to the root and you will find Meaning.

— JIANZHI SENGCAN

THE TAO AT WORK

Practice non-action.
Work without doing.
Taste the tasteless.
Magnify the small, increase the few.
Reward bitterness with care.
See simplicity in the complicated.
Achieve greatness in small things.

— 63

Most of us spend at least half of our waking life at work. Yet many people hate their jobs and wish they didn't have to go. But we have to pay our rent and put food on the table, so we accept our workday as a necessary evil. Lao Tse would see your time at work quite differently. He would suggest that the Tao can be with you throughout your workday if you are open to its presence and rewards.

Zen pundit Alan Watts put the secret of right livelihood in simple terms: "Find a way to get paid for having fun." If it strikes you as odd or impossible to get paid for having fun, you can see how doggedly you have been trained to expect the greater part of your days to be void of joy. Eight to ten or more hours per day is far too great a sacrifice to make. This is your *life* we are talking about. How, then, can you transform your workday from a drudgery into an uplifting experience?

Theologian Frederick Buechner answers thus: "To find our calling is to find the intersection between our own deep gladness and the world's deep hunger." There is something you would love to do that would make people's lives easier and for which they would be happy to pay you. Find that niche and claim it. Generate your sustenance by letting what brings you happiness become a blessing to others. If you believe you must struggle to earn a living, or you must scheme to part your customers from their shekels, you do not believe in the power of the Tao. Do not stop short of a career that makes your life better by helping others make their lives better.

Let's look at the most important elements of a Tao-based career:

1. You feel good about your day, your work, and your life.

When people go to work, they shouldn't have to leave their hearts at home.

— BETTY BENDER

Soul reward is the key element of a Tao-based job. You should wake up in the morning and look forward to your day. At the end of the day you should feel fulfilled. Obstacles may arise, but you find them stimulating, not daunting, and all of your experiences become fuel for growth. Many people do not enjoy soul satisfaction as they count the minutes until they can take their life back at the end of the workday, or mark off their calendar with the countdown to retirement like a prisoner ticks the days until release. When you are living in the Tao you do not count minutes or years. You are so immersed in the moment that time disappears. It's only when we are bored or resistant that we keep looking at the clock.

"But I have a rote job not at all connected to my passion," you state. "When I get home I am glad to leave it behind." Okay, not everyone's career represents their deepest passion. In this case, there are several ways you can keep your inner flame burning:

a. *Reframe your job so you see it in a higher light.* My coaching client Lisa wanted to leave her longtime job in a blood analysis laboratory so she could be a professional life coach. "I want to feel like I am making a difference in people's lives," she told me. When I asked her what her job entailed, she explained, "When someone with an unusual blood type is in danger of dying due to a trauma, I call around until I find a source for the blood, and I have it rushed to the hospital." Hearing that, I told Lisa, "You are saving people's lives on a daily basis, and you are trying to figure out how to make a difference? If I were one of those people who received blood due to your intervention, I would come and kiss your feet." Lisa had to laugh. "I guess I am helping people more than I thought."

Unless you are a gangster or crook, your work is helping people somehow. Step back and consider the contribution you are making, and you may discover more reward in your work than you realized.

b. *Find ways to create joyful moments at work independent of the content of the work.* Even if your work is boring, you can cultivate meaningful connections with your colleagues or customers. I often cite the toll collector who sang opera to the drivers passing through his station. No matter how bored, shut down, or grumpy your customers are, each of them is a living spirit eager to be acknowledged and stirred. Connecting with that spirit makes the difference between a dull day and an enlivening one, for you and for them. Get to know the people you serve and work with. Develop relationships. Ask your clients how their weekend was. Laugh with them. Play with them. Compliment and validate them. Support and encourage them when they feel down. Every encounter offers the potential for healing. Unwrap the gifts before you. They are there.

c. *Find ways to do things you love while working.* If your desk job allows, put on earbuds and listen to your favorite music or inspirational programming like Internet-based Hay House Radio. If you drive a truck, listen to recorded motivational talks. If you are a teacher, create uplifting projects for your students. If you are a school crossing guard, greet the kids and their parents. If you are a doctor, incorporate holistic techniques in your practice. If you sit at a security station, think about your hobby and develop creative ideas you will put into action when you get home. Don't just write off your job as a drag. Take what you have and make what you want.

d. If you have a supervisorial or entrepreneurial position, *delegate tasks you find boring or unappealing.* "If it's not fun, hire it done." Slice away what leaves your soul cold, and maximize what keeps it warm.

e. *Devote your off time to soul-fulfilling activities.* You do not need to engage in your passionate hobby eight hours a day to keep your soul alive. Play your musical instrument or build your invention when you get home. A couple of hours here and there will recharge your battery and carry you through your workday until you get a chance to once again be with what you love.

f. *Develop your passionate path while you keep your day job.* Don't wait until you quit or retire to do what you love. Start now to build the career or creative path you value. Use your free time to develop a soul-rewarding vocation. The more you invest in your passionate path, the faster it will grow and the more fulfillment you will reap. When the time is ripe, you can segue to higher ground.

Bottom line: If you are not enjoying what you are doing, either find a way to re-create or reapproach your work, or leave. Do not settle for a boring or oppressive career. Take charge of your vocation and your happiness. No one is going to kidnap you from your job and plop you into a better situation. Assume responsibility to find joy in your work and your entire life.

One spring I took a job with a wood-carver. Since I didn't have any skill in the craft, my boss gave me the task to remove the bark from some trees he had cut, preparing for him to carve totems of various deities that people worshipped. He took me out behind the shop to a large pile of logs that had been hauled in from the forest. There he gave me a knife, showed me how to scrape the bark away, and where to place the cleaned wood and bark when I was done.

The job was not hard and required no intelligence. I sat down and started husking. It was not long before my mind was wandering elsewhere. After a few hours I was quite bored. I wished I had a more interesting job that stimulated or challenged me. Every now and then the owner would bring customers behind the shop and show them the process he used to create his crafts. I said hello to them as they passed.

After a few days I was bored out of my mind. I had told the boss I would help him until the current batch of logs was processed, but when I looked at the pile I realized it would take weeks, maybe a month to finish. I wanted to quit but I needed the money. I felt trapped.

When a holiday festival came, I went to see Lao Tse. He greeted me warmly and asked how I was doing. I told him about my boring job and asked him if he thought I should quit. He told me, "You can quit if you want to. The Tao does not require anyone to struggle or suffer."

I was relieved to hear that. Immediately I began to plan my quitting speech.

Then the master continued, "But before you do, I want to show you something."

I was not surprised. Just when I thought we were heading in a direction, he would come up with, "But before you do . . ."

My mentor took me on a walk down the hill until we arrived at a large stable. Lao Tse greeted the owner, whom he knew. "Where is Lun?" the master asked.

"Check in the south stable."

I followed the master to another building where we found Lun, a thin middle-aged man with dark, leathery skin.

When he saw Lao Tse approach, he smiled and I saw he had just a few teeth. His back was bent and his clothes dirty from his work. He took his shovel, scooped one last load of horse manure, and tossed it into a wagon.

"How is it going, Lun?" asked the master.

"It's a good day," the fellow answered. "The horses are healthy, the sun is shining, and my family is fed. I am very blessed."

I was taken aback. He was the last person I would expect to be so happy.

"Do you ever have a bad day?" asked the master, almost rhetorically.

Lun smiled and shook his head. "I can't afford to. Then I would miss a moment of my life. Not worth it."

Lao Tse nodded and the two went on with some small talk. I just stood in awe, watching this man with the lowliest of positions, glowing and radiating unlike people with wealth and power.

After a while Lao Tse said good-bye to the fellow, I told him it was nice meeting him, and the master and I headed back up the hill.

As soon as we left the stable I asked Lao Tse, "Is he always that happy?"

The master smiled. "Always."

"And all he does is shovel manure?"

"That and other simple maintenance tasks."

I was at a loss for words. Here was a toothless guy with a bent back hauling dung, glowing more than most people I had ever met. I understood why Lao Tse took me to meet him.

As if reading my mind, the master said, "Jobs don't make or break our happiness. Only our mind does. Point your mind in the right direction, and you can turn any job into an adventure."

When I returned to the wood-carver's shop I felt renewed. As I took my knife and began husking the bark, I enjoyed working with the natural materials. I was happy to be outside in spring. When the boss brought customers past me, I struck up conversations and felt engaged talking with them. I was happy to have the income. Besides, I wouldn't be in this job forever. Suddenly it all became okay. I didn't want to miss a moment.

Life is not happening to you.
Life is responding to you.

— AUTHOR UNKNOWN

2. You contribute to making your customers' lives better.

Give up ingenuity, renounce profit,

And bandits and thieves will disappear.

These three are outward forms alone:
they are not sufficient in themselves.

It is more important

To see the simplicity,

To realize our true nature,

To cast off selfishness

And temper desire.

—— 19

English novelist George Eliot asked, "What are we here for if not to make each other's lives easier?" Every human being has some need, hardship, or inner battle they are fighting. If you can fill that need, lighten their hardship, or help them win their battle, you are making the best use of your vocation. A real estate salesman told me, "The turning point in my career came when I quit trying to sell real estate and I redefined my job as helping people make their dreams come true. Now I enjoy my work a lot more and I have become far more successful."

None of us can go it alone. That's why the Tao gave us each other. Your workday is as much about *how* you deliver your service as it is about the service itself. When I took a shuttle bus from an airport to a rental car agency, I found the van driver to be delightful. This woman was extraordinarily welcoming, upbeat, and helpful. She joked with the customers and made the ride a pleasure rather than the drudgery many people experience. I was so moved by the driver that I sent her manager an e-mail recounting my experience and complimenting the driver. The next time I arrived at that airport I encountered the same driver, and I told her I had sent a positive note on her behalf. Hearing that, she lit up and told me she had printed out that e-mail, framed it, and hung it on the wall of her home. The e-mail took me but a few minutes to write, but its effect extended far beyond words. The Tao is built on uplifting energy generously passed around. Good is multiplied when it is shared.

3. You feel abundant and your needs are met.

Wealth is the abiding awareness that you live in an abundant universe that is ready, willing, and able to support you to do what you need to do when you need to do it. There are an infinite number of ways providence can and will find you. Income from your job is just one of them. In other cases your sustenance may come through another channel, such as your spouse, family, the government, the kindness of people who love you, or an inheritance.

Sandra's parents divorced when she was a baby. She never knew her father or saw him again. As an adult, Sandra yearned to establish a coaching practice. She wanted to set up a studio but did not have the funds. Then Sandra received a letter informing her that her father had died and he had left her a large inheritance sufficient for her to initiate her business, and a lot more. Even though Sandra regarded herself as fatherless, her father had not forgotten her. He loved her from a distance and wanted to provide for her needs. I see Sandra's story as a metaphor: Even though we may consider ourselves unknown or uncared for, our Benefactor loves us and provides for us through often unexpected channels. Love has not abandoned you. You are not an exception to the principle of grace. You are its fulfillment.

4. You are growing spiritually.

The purpose of life is spiritual awakening, to remember who we are and live from our highest identity. Every encounter and experience exists in the service of that greater goal. When you use daily events, including your career, as a platform to advance your spiritual growth, you have passed a crucial milestone on your journey.

You can tell that a plant is healthy when it shows new growth. Likewise, your career should regularly be sending out new shoots. You should be getting new ideas and exploring wider avenues for you to express your creativity, revel in your work, and improve your customers' lives. If you are not regenerating, you are degenerating. If you are not composing, you are decomposing. If your work is not particularly exciting, you should be sending out new shoots in your personal life. You have to be growing in some facet of your experience. Many people slip into a rut and then wonder why they are not happy. Educator Laurence J. Peter said, "A rut is a grave with the ends knocked out." It is tempting to keep doing the same thing in the same way, especially if your routine is creating an income stream. But there are deeper streams that will make your life more meaningful and also enhance your income. If you feel flat or empty in your career, ask yourself, "What can I do to keep my life force moving?" Use your imagination and think creatively. Even an inkling of enthusiasm is your guide to the next step that will yield you soul reward and greater prosperity. Trust joy as the voice of the Tao, act on it, and you will attract all the means you need to advance.

5. You make challenges work in your favor.

A master of the Tao does not shy away from challenges. When they show up, she accepts them and asks, "What is the opportunity behind this apparent difficulty?" Setbacks are really setups to advance. Every challenge helps you build a muscle that will serve you far more than if the challenge had not occurred. The greater the challenge, the greater the opportunity for transformation. A caller on my radio show reported, "I feel like I am on the edge of chaos." I told her, "Actually, you are on the edge of transformation." Sometimes things have to fall apart before they can come together better. Every difficulty comes with guidance to move in a new direction. Redefine challenge as your friend, and it will prove itself to be so.

6. You do no harm.

Taoist, Buddhist, and (intrinsically pure) Christian teachings, as well as other spiritual paths, underscore the importance of not causing pain to others. If your work is hurting someone in any way, it is moving against the Tao and will not succeed. If your winning depends on someone else losing, you have both lost.

Here are examples of industries or actions that cause harm and violate the Tao:

- Manufacturing or selling chemical products that make people or the environment sick, such as toxic fertilizers, pesticides, preservatives, pollutants, or drugs that foster addictions or produce caustic side effects

- Creating false needs, engendering a sense of lack, and preying upon consumers' fears to entice them to buy a product

- Pumping up illusions that teach consumers, especially children, that they will become attractive, powerful, and lovable if they conform to a certain body image, income rank, or social status

- Producing violence-filled movies, video games, music, and sports that incite viewers or listeners to act out violence

- Luring consumers to establish debts that will burden them; selling mortgages at subprime rates that lead to economic collapse

- Engaging in politics that deny citizens their equality, well-being, freedom, or human rights

- Amassing far more money than you need as an individual or corporation and not returning a portion to the community for charity or service

Better stop short than fill to the brim.
Oversharpen the blade, and the edge will soon blunt.
Amass a store of gold and jade, and no one can protect it.
Claim wealth and titles, and disaster will follow.

— 9

- Devoting the greater portion of a nation's income to war or war materials; manufacturing or selling products to profit from war

- Manipulating living beings to engage in demeaning behaviors for personal profit or pleasure, such as pedophilia, child pornography, sex trafficking, factory farms or laboratory testing that treat animals inhumanely, poaching endangered species, or enslaving animals for circus shows

- Hunting for sport rather than food

While there are many more items we could add to this list, you can understand from these examples why so many people are in psychic and physical pain. A significant sector of suffering-inducing commerce is accepted as normal, sanctioned, and even encouraged. You can help reduce unethical commerce by not working in such industries or purchasing their products, and by participating in political activities to prohibit offensive practices. Anything you do personally or commercially that is aligned with the Tao will help diminish pain in the world. Mahatma Gandhi said, "The pure love of one person can offset the hatred of millions." Never underestimate the power of kindness, service, and integrity. Those virtues will never fail you or those you touch.

You may believe that your job is the activity you go to each day to earn income. Your real job is to live in harmony with the Tao. Don't write off your time at work as meaningless or a hollow requirement. Don't waste your precious minutes in boredom or complaint. Every moment is an invitation to unveil the riches with which you have been endowed. Create reward throughout your day and bless yourself and the people you touch by remembering that wherever you stand, you are in the presence of love. When you accept that invitation, you go beyond making a living to make a life.

The pieces of a chariot are useless
unless they work in accordance with the whole.
A man's life brings nothing
unless he lives in accordance with the whole universe.
Playing one's part
in accordance with the universe
is true humility.

— 39

WHAT MAKES
LEADERS GREAT

The more laws and restrictions there are,

The poorer people become.

The sharper men's weapons,

The more trouble in the land . . .

The more rules and regulations,

The more thieves and robbers.

Therefore the wise one says:

"I take no action and people behave themselves.

I enjoy peace and people become honest.

I do nothing and people become rich.

*I have no desires and people return to the
good and simple life."*

—— 57

When I saw an ad for a "You Fly" air tour of three Hawaiian islands, my heart leaped. It had been my longtime dream to fly an airplane, and this excursion would allow me to take the stick of the craft for a little while as I soared over paradise. I signed up and eagerly anticipated my few moments of glory.

I met my pilot Scott at the Maui airport, where he walked me to a twin-engine Cessna and gave me a brief rundown about the various instruments on the control panel. Scott buckled himself into the seat next to mine and told me, "Now here's how you take off . . ."

Excuse me, I thought, *I don't remember the advertisement saying anything about taking off.* I started to say, "Perhaps you didn't hear me say I've never flown before." But when I looked over at Scott he was on the radio setting up our takeoff with the control tower. Then I understood what was happening: *He thought I could do it.* To Scott, taking off was not too much to ask of me. So I kept my mouth shut. I decided to believe in Scott's belief in my ability. I followed his careful instructions, and within a few minutes we were airborne.

I flew the airplane nearly three hours that day. I flew over the dramatic north shore of Maui, past the thousand-foot sweeping cliffs of Molokai, across the golden sand beaches of Lanai, then over whales and dolphins cavorting in the channel back to Maui. With me mostly piloting and Scott stepping in for an occasional correction, my nervousness gave way to exhilaration, and my doubts yielded to confidence.

As we made our way back to the airport, Scott surprised me again. "Now here's how you land," he told me nonchalantly. *Now wait just a minute,* I felt like saying. *Taking off and flying is one thing, but landing—now that's outright dangerous.* Then I remembered a lesson from one of my favorite flyers, Richard Bach, who said, "Argue for your limits, and sure enough they're yours." Again I denied my impulse to resist.

As I guided us in according to Scott's instructions, a huge gust of wind rocked the tiny aircraft. "Sure is windy here," Scott laughed. "Maui's airport is one of the windiest anywhere." Yow! *Okay, just breathe.* I kept following Scott's directions until he took over before touchdown.

As I left the airport that day, I felt higher than our flight. Scott's belief in me brought out the best in me. The flight was three hours; the lesson was for a lifetime.

There are two kinds of leaders: those who tell people what to do, and those who show people what to do. Those who guide by command, and those who inspire by example. Those who use their position to control others, and those who empower their followers. Genuine leaders do not seize glory. They give it to those they lead.

> *If you would guide the people, you must serve with humility.*
>
> *If you would lead them, you must follow behind.*
>
> — 66

In *Tao Te Ching*, Lao Tse offers a great deal of advice to leaders. While at first it appears that the master is illuminating the secrets to rule a nation, he is more specifically teaching us how to rule our lives. Know it or not, like it or not, you are a leader. Every day you make a thousand decisions that steer your life and affect every person you meet by your energy, actions, and model. When you know how to lead your life, you will help others to lead theirs.

Let us penetrate to the heart of Lao Tse's insight into what makes leaders great:

1. Service above Self

We must ask of any person seeking leadership, *Do you truly wish to help others, or is your quest for position an ego trip? Are you here to make the world a better place, or to fortify your own kingdom?* We don't have to look very far to see politicians and business moguls who care little for the masses, but rather seek to puff their profile, line their pockets, or cater to special interest groups. In our era anyone can get elected or appointed, even people of despicable character. Individuals without ethics or compassion can also rise to altitude in business and religion. Unscrupulous leaders may have their day, but sooner or later the Tao will pluck them from office because they have betrayed integrity. What is of the Tao endures; what is not perishes.

Genuine leaders exert their influence in loci far beyond public office. In the inspiring documentary series *The Kindness*

Diaries, adventurist Leon Logothetis journeys around the globe to discover acts of service and reward them. He travels first across America, then Europe and Asia, with no money, and depends entirely on the generosity of good-hearted people to help him eat, sleep, and fuel his cranky old motorcycle. Many people turn Leon down, but everywhere he goes he encounters some people who are more interested in taking care of others than protecting themselves. In Los Angeles, Leon met a homeless man who gave him all of the few possessions he had. In Turkey, a generous fellow arranged a flight on a cargo plane to help Leon get to India without having to drive through war-endangered Iran and Pakistan. In India, a father struggling to feed his family gave Leon his bed while he slept on the floor. In Vietnam, Leon found a surgeon who performs cataract-removal operations for people who cannot afford them. Dr. Vu Xuan Nguyen has saved the sight of thousands of people at no charge, functioning on donations only. Dr. Nguyen's face radiates a peace I have never seen on people who work for money, fame, or position only. Behold genuine leadership without fanfare or ego. Albert Schweitzer noted, "The only ones among you who will be really happy are those who will have sought and found how to serve."

> *The wise stay behind, and are thus ahead.*
> *They are detached, thus at one with all.*
> *Through selfless action, they attain fulfillment.*
>
> *— 7*

2. Transparency

Sincere leaders have nothing to hide. Because they are in integrity with themselves, their constituents, and their mission, they can stand naked without fear of injury. Candor is so rare among people in high positions that when we hear one speak authentically, their honesty resonates like a clear bell. I saw an interview with Princess Diana after her divorce. She courageously revealed the truth about her marriage, extramarital affair, eating disorder, and her love-hate experience in royalty. While some would argue that Diana's radical honesty made her vulnerable, it actually made her believable, endearing, and invincible. *A Course in Miracles* asks us to remember, "In my defenselessness my safety lies."

> *The weak can overcome the strong;*
> *The supple can overcome the stiff.*
> *Under heaven everyone knows this,*
> *Yet no one puts it into practice.*
> *Therefore the wise say:*
> *"If you take on the humiliation of the people,*
> *you are fit to rule them.*
> *If you take upon yourself the country's disasters,*
> *You deserve to be ruler of the universe."*
> *The truth often sounds paradoxical.*
>
> — 78

3. Walking the Talk

A mother brought her six-year-old son to Mahatma Gandhi and asked the acclaimed emancipator to tell her son to stop eating sugar. Gandhi instructed the woman to come back with the boy in a week. When she did, Gandhi told him, "Stop eating sugar."

"Why didn't you just tell my son that last week?" the mother asked.

"Because last week I was still eating sugar."

Genuine leaders bear authority because they do what they ask others to do. It's easy to spout rhetoric and tell other people how to live. It is harder to live the principles we wish others would practice. When we step back from bossing the world and we walk the talk we profess, our leadership is empowered by the unimpeachable alignment of our words and deeds.

Therefore the wise work without recognition.
They achieve what has to be done without dwelling on it.
They do not try to show their knowledge.
— 77

Example is not the main thing in influencing others.
It is the only thing.
— ALBERT SCHWEITZER

4. Inclusion and Equality

One can discern between authentic leaders and imposters by observing their level of inclusiveness. Do they care for all people, or just a select few? Do they believe that all of their constituents deserve freedom, abundance, and empowerment, or just members of their elite club? Do they dole out benefits to the masses, or do they slice away groups with traits they judge against? There is no caste system in the kingdom of heaven. All are welcome and all deserve blessing. Wise leaders embrace. Deluded leaders divide.

Therefore the wise take care of everyone
And abandon no one.
They take care of all things
And abandon nothing.
This is called "following the light."
— 27

The wise do not hold opinions.
They are aware of the needs of others.
I am good to people who are good.
I am also good to people who are not good,
Because Virtue is goodness.
I have faith in people who are faithful.
I also have faith in people who are not faithful,
Because Virtue is faithfulness.

— 49

5. Nonviolence

Lao Tse identifies the Tao as the force behind all healing and success. There is another attempted force that opposes the Tao—ego-based acts of aggression, bullying, manipulation, and guilt-based pressure. On a personal level we intimidate, threaten, pull rank, shout, sabotage, punish, injure, and murder. As a nation we brag, show off weapons, exercise military action, dominate, invade, build bigger bombs, and commit genocide. While such personal and national aggression may temporarily gain the illusion of power, ultimately it must implode. What is not of the Tao leads to the abyss. *A Course in Miracles* tells us that the world "is totally insane and leads nowhere."

Whenever you advise rulers in the way of Tao,
Counsel them not to use force to conquer the universe.
For this would only cause resistance.
Thorn bushes spring up wherever the army has passed.
Lean years follow in the wake of a great war.
Just do what needs to be done.
Never take advantage of power . . .

Achieve results,
But not through violence.
Force is followed by loss of strength.
This is not the way of the Tao.
That which goes against the Tao
Comes to an early end.

— 30

Finally the master put it bluntly:

"A violent person will die a violent death!"
This is the essence of my teaching.

— 42

6. Unpretentiousness

A true leader identifies with the masses and merges into the purpose of the group she represents. Minor attention should be paid to the leader as a person, and major attention to the goals of the organization. Leaders who draw attention to themselves as individuals rather than the vision they serve have been hijacked by ego.

Mahatma Gandhi is an exemplar of a modest yet supremely effective leader. Wearing but a loincloth, sitting on straw mats, eschewing possessions, and seeking to unite warring religious factions, he liberated one of the most populated nations on Earth in a gentle way. He did not seek to shine the spotlight on himself as an individual. His purpose was to serve his country and his people.

Warren Buffett, one of the world's most successful business leaders, conducts an unaffected life. With many billions of dollars to his name, he lives in a normal house in a suburban neighborhood, drives an older car, sometimes flies coach (even though he owns an airline), and is regularly seen at local theater plays and ice-cream shops. He gave two of his children a billion dollars each on the condition that they donate it to charity. I once phoned Warren Buffett's office on behalf of a friend who wanted to invite him to speak at a conference. I got through to his personal secretary who assured me that Mr. Buffett would get the message and respond. Warren Buffett has not been seduced by the trappings of fame and fortune. He has remained a real and available person, and levels the playing field to meet everyone on common ground.

Loving the people and ruling the country,

Can you be without cleverness?

Opening and closing the gates of heaven,

Can you play the role of woman?

Understanding and being open to all things,

Are you able to do nothing?

Giving birth and nourishing,

Bearing yet not possessing,

Working yet not taking credit,

Leading yet not dominating,

This is the Primal Virtue.

— 10

As we approached the governor's mansion, my stomach dropped out. Rumors of executions and excommunications issuing from this compound had rippled through the province for years. I tried to fathom why Lao Tse had been called here. He was widely known as a freethinker, and he may very well have been summoned for interrogation and assassination. I had been often seen with him, and the powers that be could easily do away with me as well.

Neither had I ever seen Lao Tse enter such an ostentatious domain. He hardly ever associated with rich or influential people. He was at home with earthy peasants, devoid of social status or pretense, living in the simplest of homes. He had often spoken of the trappings of worldly power and possessions.

A guard stopped us at the door. Lao Tse introduced himself, and the guard recognized his name. The guard bowed his head, opened the door, and bid us enter.

If I had felt intimidated when I first saw the mansion, I was much more so now. Expensive, exotic artwork adorned the walls, set off by finely crafted teak tables displaying gold-trimmed dinner bowls and artisan-crafted chopsticks. A collection of rare and ancient swords hung proudly on the wall. Had I entered some museum boasting medals of the conquest of nations?

A woman, mid-40s, approached us. She was pretty, but her face was haggard and her elegant clothing disheveled. My eyes were drawn to some stains on her sleeve that looked like blood.

"You must be Lao Tse," she said, looking hopeful.

The master bowed.

"I am Tang Sai'er, the governor's wife. Please, come in. He wants to see you."

I felt my solar plexus unclench. This was no inquisition. What else could we be here for?

Tang Sai'er escorted us up a staircase to an imposing wooden door flanked by two swarthy guards. One of them opened the door to reveal a large bedroom. Several official-looking men were hovering around a bed. Seeing us enter, they parted. There, lying in bed I saw a middle-aged man with a salt-and-pepper beard, his skin very pale. His head rested on a large pillow, his eyes staring at the ceiling.

"Lao Tse is here," Tang Sai'er announced, a lilt of relief in her voice.

A slight smile spread over the man's face. He lifted his head a bit, but, in pain, it soon dropped back. The patient, obviously the governor, motioned for Lao Tse to come closer. The master prodded me on the lower back to follow him.

"I've been waiting to meet you for a long time," the governor said.

Lao Tse bowed his head, stepped toward the bed, and sat at the man's hip.

"Two nights ago I went out behind the house to take a piss," he said, his voice strained. "Two thugs were waiting in the bushes. One grabbed me and the other stuck a knife in my gut. My guards heard me yell and ran out. The bastards got away." The governor winced. "I have lost a lot of blood and my doctor tells me my liver is gone. I am all infected. There is no hope. I will not see the morning sun."

My body tensed as I realized the gravity of the situation.

The governor grabbed the master's forearm. "I have been hearing of your teachings for years, Lao Tse. You know things other people do not know. Tell me straight. Will I go right to hell, or is there any hope for me to find some kind of heaven?"

Lao Tse's eyes remained steadfast on the governor. He gently placed his hand on the man's forearm. "The Tao is merciful, sir. You will return to the source of all things. Your essence will live on."

A tiny bit of color returned to the man's face. He looked more at peace. His wife began to weep.

"I have been a terrible person, Lao Tse. Surely you are aware of my reputation. I have sent many men to their death. Will I not be punished?"

"You have already been punished," the master replied. "You have lived in hell even while you walked the earth. Now your body is decimated. If you return again, you will have an opportunity to correct your mistakes. The Tao balances all things."

The governor nodded, a bittersweet look on his face. He closed his eyes and let his head sink into the pillow. I thought he had died, but when I saw his chest rise again I realized he had fallen into sleep.

Lao Tse slowly rose, turned, and made his way toward the door. I followed.

Tang Sai'er scurried to catch us and clutched the master's arm. "Thank you for coming," she said, tears streaming down her cheeks. "Is there anything I can do to obtain mercy for my husband's soul?"

"After he dies, sell his possessions and buy food for poor people," Lao Tse answered firmly. "Thus he will gain merit and his memory will be redeemed."

The woman nodded. She understood.

We left the mansion and started back toward town. After a few minutes of walking silently, the master asked me, "Have you heard of Xiao Jia?"

I thought for a moment. "He is the governor of Liang Province, isn't he?"

Lao Tse nodded. "Do you know how old he is?"

I shrugged my shoulders.

"He is approaching 75. He has ruled for over 30 years. He is beloved of his people."

"Because?"

"Because he does not consider himself the ruler. He allows the Tao to rule through him. He recognizes that he is in office only to help people. As a result, he is honored, safe, and lives a long and fruitful life."

After seeing the governor on the brink of death, the lesson sank in.

"Everyone is your teacher," the master went on. "The few rulers who follow the Tao are teachers of virtue. Strive to emulate them. Rulers who govern with an iron hand may amass the illusion of power and glory, but eventually the Tao achieves correction. It is only a matter of time. The balancing power of the Tao makes no exceptions. Evil rulers may have their day in the sun, but justice will eventually cut them down. Pride always gives way to humiliation. Observe well, my friend. The strength of a true leader is humility. Arrogance surely leads to annihilation."

We are born gentle and weak, but at death are
stiff and hard.

Green plants are tender and filled with sap.

At their death they are withered and dry.

Therefore the stiff and unbending is the disciple of death.

The gentle and yielding is the disciple of life.

Thus an army without flexibility never wins a battle.

A tree that is unbending is easily broken.

The hard and strong will fall.

The soft and weak will overcome.

— 76

7. Connection to Tao

Effective leaders understand that they do not lead by themselves. They recognize the presence and power of a Source greater than the human mind or personality, and they work in partnership with that infinite resource; their leadership is a co-creation. A friend of mine interviewed a number of successful CEOs to determine what they know and do that sets them above the crowd. Most of these influential people acknowledged their relationship with a Higher Power. My friend also discovered that people in entry-level and middle-management positions did not generally have the same relationship with their inner Source. The higher up in rank the interviewee, the more the executives worked with help from above.

> *Really great men have a curious feeling that the greatness is not of them, but through them. And they see something divine in every other man and are endlessly, foolishly, incredibly merciful.*
>
> — JOHN RUSKIN

Be the Leader You Seek

While it is tempting to hope that leaders will save us, we cannot afford to wait for high-profile officials to walk the Great Way. We must walk it ourselves and influence by our model. Government is not causational; it is an effect of the people who elect it in democracies or put up with it in dictatorships. It's easy to criticize leaders for their lack of integrity; we have no shortage of examples. Yet our first responsibility is to remove the weeds from our own garden. We must take the high road ourselves before exhorting others to do so.

> *Mastering others requires force;*
> *mastering the self needs strength.*
>
> — 33

Positive leadership is achieved by building a foundation of virtue within the masses. A healthy nation grows from the ground up. A friend of mine traveled to vacation in Hawaii and flew late at night into the wrong airport, two hours from her hotel. When she went to pick up her rental car, the agent was very sympathetic. Although my friend's booking was for another outlet, the agent gave her a car from that station's inventory and took meticulous time to tell my friend how to get to the hotel in the dark and avoid bad road conditions and construction zones. The next day the agent phoned my friend at her hotel to make sure she had arrived safely. Such an agent, while not very high in the corporate hierarchy, was doing more good for that company than an executive focused solely on increasing company profits. She was teaching kindness by her example, making her a world-class leader in her own right—as each of us can and must be.

The Parting of the Ways

A spiritual teacher explained that the world has reached a parting of the ways. "Imagine two trains leaving a train station at the same time, each heading in a slightly different direction," he suggested. "At first the trains are not very far apart. If you wished to jump from one to the other, you could do so without much difficulty. As the trains continue on their trajectories, the distance between them increases. For a while you might still achieve a transfer, but that jump rapidly becomes farther and harder. At some point the trains will be so far apart that it will be impossible to change. You must choose one or the other."

Recent political events have stunningly demonstrated this dynamic. We are now experiencing two radically different realities, with no middle ground. Such a critical juncture calls each of us to look into our heart, choose what we truly believe, and live those principles. The two belief systems currently before us represent the contrast between dark and light; selfishness or service; separation or inclusion; hate or love.

Recognizing the eternal truths that govern life, Lao Tse long ago gave the answer to our current predicament:

The clarity of the sky prevents it from falling.

The firmness of the earth prevents it from splitting.

The strength of the spirit prevents it from being exhausted.

The fullness of the valley prevents it from drying up.

The growth of the ten thousand things prevents their extinction.

Good leadership by those in power prevents the country from failing.

— 39

Think less about how your leaders are leading your world, and more about how you are leading your life. Our leaders reflect our consciousness. While there are steps we can take to improve our leaders, the first step is to upgrade our own walk. When we live in the Tao we attract leaders who lead from the Tao. Your power to change the world begins with your power to change yourself. What is within you is greater than what is around you. Lao Tse claimed that power 2,500 years ago, and we must each claim it now.

If you preserve your original qualities,

you can govern anything.

— 28

TECHNOLOGY
AND SANITY

*Though there are machines that can work ten
to a hundred times faster than people,
they are not needed.*

—— 80

During Theodore Roosevelt's presidency, a group of developers wanted to turn the Grand Canyon into a Disneyland-like theme park. Roosevelt journeyed to the rim of the canyon, drank in the stunning view, and stated, "Leave it as it is. You cannot improve on it. The ages have been at work on it and man can only mar it."

During the century since Roosevelt uttered that advice, we have manufactured countless inventions to improve on nature. Yet after a steady progression of ever-more sophisticated machines, one must wonder if technology has improved the quality of life on earth or undermined it. A recent survey revealed that Americans are less happy than they were 70 years ago. While machines have in many ways made our lives easier, they have not made us happier. They have increased the speed of our life, but have not increased the quality of our life. When someone asked His Holiness the Dalai Lama, "What is your opinion of technology?" he replied, "Technology is wonderful, as long as you remain its master and do not become its slave."

We are all well aware of the miraculous ways that computer, wireless, Internet, and mobile technologies have made our lives staggeringly more efficient. They have made formerly long and laborious tasks quicker and easier, enabled us to communicate with just about anyone on the planet instantly, provided medical tools that enable us to live healthier and longer, and utterly revolutionized the way we do business. If someone who lived just a few generations ago were to return and observe the intricate instruments we now take for granted, that person's head would spin in astonishment. Used wisely, technology makes the earth more like heaven.

Used foolishly, technology turns life to hell. A young couple in South Korea was sent to prison because they were so busy playing video games that they allowed their baby daughter to starve to death. In that country and China, some people are so addicted to video games that they wear diapers so they do not have to go to the bathroom and lose points while away from the screen. One player had his leg amputated because he sat at a computer so long that he lost blood flow to his legs. The leading cause of teenage death in the U.S. is texting while driving. Such tragic events occur when human beings allow technology to override sanity. Technology was created to enhance life, not destroy it.

Keeping to the main road is easy,

But people are easily distracted.

— 53

Crafty Plans and Strange Outcomes

In our fever to keep up with the latest gadgets and apps, we overlook two crucial questions: (1) How much do I really need? and (2) Is the way I am using technology enhancing the quality of my life or detracting from it?

Lao Tse tells us that we already have everything we need to be happy. That sounds completely crazy in a world bent on *more, faster, more, faster, more.* Technology would be a better friend were we not so addicted to it. I wonder what our civilization would do if for an hour or a day or forever, LCD screens and wireless signals were not available. I fear that many people would have psychotic breaks, unable to function without their computer or mobile device. A friend of mine works on the Alaska pipeline with a group of millennial technicians. He said that these fellows are absolutely brilliant at what they do. But if they lose their wireless signal for texting and social media, they are helpless. I worry that humans are fast losing our ability to communicate face-to-face; interpersonal relationship skills are atrophying at an exponential rate. I walked into a juice bar in Southern California to find 15 of the 16 patrons immersed in their smartphones. Everyone standing in line waiting for their takeout order; a couple on a date; three teenage girls; a mother sitting with her eight-year-old son; and a guy and his pregnant wife, among other customers, were all fingering LCD screens. Except for the moment they paid the cashier, not one person in the room was looking at another person or having a conversation with a present human being. The only person not chained to a wireless device was the eight-year-old boy just waiting for his mother to look at him. I wondered if I had slipped into some bizarre *Twilight Zone* episode where the humans of Earth had become possessed by their handheld instruments. What will happen to the baby in the womb of those parents who failed to make eye contact with each other? I have a friend who used to volunteer at a hospital where she held and cuddled babies of mothers addicted to crack. Will our future require volunteers to cuddle babies whose parents are more used to touching an LCD screen than a person? My parents lived during the era before it was acknowledged that a pregnant woman drinking alcohol and smoking deleteriously affects her baby in utero. Will the next generation reveal that constant exposure to wireless signals works against a baby's health? Will the next wave of children know there is a world beyond the screen at hand? A 2002 Gallup Poll asked respondents, "How many close friends do you have?" The average answer was 10. The same poll taken recently revealed that most people have two close friends. A large number of Facebook friends does not fill our hunger for intimacy, and posting photos of lunch does not constitute communication. While technology supposedly connects us, when used improperly it disconnects us.

These are real issues we must address if we are to reclaim the wonder and reward of the Tao. I sometimes work in Japan, a culture even deeper into the techno-jungle than America. In that country, sex, relationships, and marriage are disappearing faster than you can download the latest iPhone update. Many people continue to live at home with their parents through their 30s, 40s, and even into their 50s. Twenty-five percent of people at age 30 are still virgins. Some (non-transvestite) men wear bras, disappear into anime, and develop intimate relationships with blow-up dolls. Many romances progress at a snail's pace if at all; some people date once a month for several years before they consider themselves in a serious relationship. Everyone wants their soul mate but few know how to connect or communicate. Sex is never discussed in public. As the birth rate declines, the government does not know how it is going to find the money to pay out Social Security disbursements. The Japanese culture is inherently deeply spiritual and highly moral. The people are extraordinarily kind and respectful. Technology is beginning to eclipse their capacity to enjoy warm and loving human relationships. Are we headed in the same direction?

The more ingenious and clever people are,

The more strange things happen.

—— 57

One day as Lao Tse was about to leave for the market, he asked me if I would harvest some turnips from his garden. Sure, I told him, I would be happy to.

I found a small tool and started to dig up the tubers. But eventually I had to push my hands deep into the dirt to pull out the root vegetable. The soil was muddy after an overnight rain, and I felt annoyed at how dirty my hands were getting. I also had to squat to do the work, which became uncomfortable.

It occurred to me that I could avoid dirt and squatting if I had a more efficient tool. So I took a saw and hiked into the forest just below the master's house. There I found a large old nanmu tree with a long, thick, straight branch. I cut the limb, took it back to the house, and chiseled away at one end until it formed a kind of spade I could wedge into the soil. This would allow me to get at the root without bending over or getting my hands dirty. The chiseling took me several hours, but I finally got it shaped. I went out to the garden and began to poke around the turnips.

Just then the master arrived home. "What's that?" he asked as he observed my implement.

"It's a tool I made to harvest the turnips," I answered proudly. I showed him how I was picking at the soil. "Look, I don't have to squat and get dirty."

Lao Tse quietly studied my method, his hand slowly stroking his thin gray beard.

"Your invention reminds me of the people I used to work with in the government," he finally said.

I stopped digging and turned to the master. "How's that?"

"None of them wanted to get their hands dirty. They spent all their days in offices, arguing over politics and money and bossing people around. They were the most miserable people I have ever met, abominably disconnected from the Tao. I left my post because I couldn't work in that environment anymore."

I was confused. I thought my tool was a good idea. "So I should get my hands dirty and kneel?"

"Touching the earth is healing," he replied as he leaned over to scoop up some soil with his hands and let it crumble through his fingers. "It gets you out of your head and grounds you. Gardeners and farmers are among the happiest people because they stay connected to the Tao by constantly touching living things."

I gripped my tool. "What's wrong with standing?"

"There's nothing wrong with it. But when you squat or kneel, you move more life force through your body. Such movement will keep you healthier longer."

I still felt defensive after spending all that time and effort to fashion my tool. "What am I supposed to do about my dirty hands?"

> "Come with me," said the master. He led me to a little brook 20 paces to the east, effervescent and swollen from the rain. There he kneeled and rinsed his hands. "Washing your hands in the brook is also healing. Moving water contains huge chi. The same rain that made the garden muddy has given you a way to cleanse the dirt. All elements of the Tao work together."
>
> I could feel my argument crumbling.
>
> Lao Tse stood and shook his hands of the excess water. "It's fine to make tools that make our life easier. Just be careful not to make your life so easy that you separate yourself from the Tao. Then your life will be harder."

Lo! Men have become the tools of their tools.

— HENRY DAVID THOREAU

Fiction Closer to Fact

I saw a science-fiction film in which an alien race had so lost themselves in their technology that they grew devoid of all feeling, became infertile, and quit reproducing, until the species was on the brink of extinction. So the extraterrestrials traveled to Earth, where people still felt deeply, embodied passion, and related to each other as living beings rather than machines. The aliens extracted human genetic material and implanted it in their own species as their last hope of survival. This procedure explained the rash of alien abductions in which human beings were taken onto spacecraft and had their genitals probed. While the story is presented as fiction, it may be prophetic in its warning that if we give our power away to technology and lose touch with our humanity, we may cancel ourselves out of existence. The journal *Human Reproduction* reported that in England, infertility affects one out of six couples, and sperm count in British males has dropped by nearly half in the past 60 years. In 40 percent of infertility cases, doctors cannot explain the couple's inability to conceive. In

America, in vitro fertilization has increased by 63 percent since 2003. While infertility certainly cannot be attributed simply to technology addiction, it may be related indirectly. Toxic chemicals in food and the environment may be one factor, and loss of libido after sitting in front of an LCD screen for eight or more hours a day without exercise may be another. In fairness to technology, we may rightfully applaud that in vitro fertilization is a beneficial result of advanced science. But wouldn't it be more natural, fun, and far less expensive and complicated to just create babies the old-fashioned way?

Digitization has become a substitute for human experience. People would rather photograph the sunset than savor it; strike up fantasy cyber-relationships in which partners never meet in person; or ride in a driverless taxi rather than interact with a living person who might interrupt them from texting. (Some of the most rewarding conversations of my life have been with taxi drivers.) A recent survey revealed that 10 percent of people check their smartphones while they are having sex, and 35 percent do so immediately afterward. I saw a sign in the hallway of an apartment building: "In case of fire, exit the building before posting the event on social media." Swiss playwright and novelist Max Frisch has defined technology as "the knack of so arranging the world that we don't have to experience it."

When we distance ourselves from what is natural, life goes sideways. What is of the Tao proliferates. What is not of the Tao fades into nothingness. This is the Tao's fail-safe to perpetuate life as creation intended.

What is firmly established cannot be uprooted.

What is firmly grasped cannot slip away.

It will be honored from generation to generation.

—— 54

The Gifts We Already Own

Lao Tse would suggest that the way to avoid tumbling down the techno-hypnosis rabbit hole is to recognize that the Tao has already implanted within us all the technology we need to live happy, healthy, productive lives. The marvelously efficient devices we have developed simply replicate our innate faculties that have atrophied due to disuse. We all have psychic abilities that enable us to communicate with each other over vast distances. Ocean voyagers have been navigating by way of the stars and currents for thousands of years. We can calculate complex equations with our minds. I used to work with developmentally disabled adults. One fellow, Mack, was a savant (like the based-on-true character Rain Man). One day while Mack was waiting for the bus to take him home, he asked me the date and year of my birth. When I told him, he instantly replied, "That was a Tuesday." He was correct. I was stunned. The fellow could not dress himself, but he could immediately identify the weekday of any date in recent history. Autistic Daniel Tammet calculated the value of pi to 22,514 decimal places without using a calculator, and he learns new languages in a week. I was floored to watch a video of Stephen Wiltshire, another autistic man, who displays impeccable photographic memory. Researchers took Wiltshire on a short helicopter ride over the city of Rome. Then they placed him in a room with a 17-foot-wide whiteboard and asked him to draw what he had seen. Three days later Stephen completed a nearly perfect sketch of the entire city of Rome, down to the minutest detail, including every column in the Pantheon. He has replicated this astounding feat in several other large cities. Mack's, Tammet's, and Wiltshire's amazing faculties demonstrate that the human brain has the capacity to do everything computers do for us. While these people's abilities are extraordinary in practice, they represent a potential we all own. We could navigate our entire lives without sophisticated technology if we needed to. The Tao has already endowed us with all the powers with which we have endowed computers. We play God with our computers the way God has played God with us. If we realized that we already embody the technology we seek, we would not need to invent machines to replace ourselves.

Prophets at Large

While psychic knowing or prophecy is a gift we believe is bestowed upon a chosen few, we are all innately psychic. Dr. Roger D. Nelson of Princeton University has spent more than 20 years developing the Global Consciousness Project (GCP), using random number generators to detect strong waves of feelings in masses of human beings. When this machine is influenced by intense emotional energy, the sequencing stops being random and falls into patterns. Dr. Nelson's team has placed 70 random number generators around the globe to see if they can detect trends in the group mind and emotions of humanity. The researchers discovered that on September 11, 2001, the day of terrorist attacks on the U.S., the random number generators registered a huge spike in emotional energy around the globe four hours *before* the planes crashed into the Twin Towers. The GCP also found precognitive spikes associated with globally significant events like the death of Princess Diana in 1997 and the 2004 Indian Ocean tsunami. Somewhere in the collective consciousness of human beings, we sense when a significant event is about to occur, and we generate mass emotional ripples as a result. Not only are we psychic as individuals, but we have collective knowingness as humanity. Spiritual teachers have been telling us for millennia that all minds are joined. Now science is demonstrating this profound capacity.

Living in the Supernatural

What we call supernatural is really natural. What we call paranormal is really normal. What we call extrasensory is really sensory. All of these faculties that we have for so long believed to be beyond our capacity are *within* our capacity. You are now being called to be who you were created to be before you created yourself to be otherwise. If Lao Tse lived today, I imagine he might have a smartphone, but he would own it rather than it owning him. He would regard it as a toy or a helpful tool rather than a necessity. He would play with it rather than letting it play him. He could live with it, but he could live without it. If we can step into the same level of mastery, we will enjoy our right place in the Grand Design.

Technology is the sharpest two-edged sword that humanity has ever wielded. Medicine can snatch souls from the jaws of death, while the military can send hundreds of thousands to the grave with a touch of a button. The Internet makes the sum of human knowledge available to all humanity, and simultaneously provides a venue for hate to reach around the globe to strangle goodness. Satellites feed GPS devices that enable us to rapidly reach our destinations, while some drivers never arrive because they are watching their phones rather than the road. The chemicals that keep our foods on the shelf longer keep our bodies on the planet shorter. Technology, for better and worse, is not our problem. Our problem is that knowledge is advancing faster than the wisdom to use it. Data transfer is racing beyond our spiritual maturity. We must figure out how to use our machines in the *service* of the Tao rather than *against* it. We must catch our integrity up to our scientific savvy. Science is a blessing to the wise and a curse to the ignorant. We do not need more machines. We need more consciousness. We must be at choice about whether we will control our devices or they will control us. Ultimately we do not need them. What we need is to understand why we are here and what makes our life worthwhile.

Do you think you can conquer the universe and
improve it?

I do not believe this can be done.

The universe is sacred.

You cannot improve it.

If you try to change it, you will ruin it.

If you try to hold on to it, you will lose it.

—— 29

MAKE PEACE
WITH YOUR BODY

Carrying body and soul and embracing the one,
Can you avoid separation?
Attending fully and becoming supple,
Can you be as a newborn babe?
— 10

The moment you arrived on Earth you received a body. Then you spent the rest of your life trying to figure out what to do with it. After existing as an infinite, limitless, self-sufficient spirit, in a flash you were squeezed into a little package with all kinds of needs you could not control. You became dependent on other people and external commodities for your safety and survival. As time went on, you began to think of yourself as less and less of a spirit and more and more of a body. At some point you forgot the realm of light you came from and you came to believe that you are trapped in a world of seven billion other bodies competing for limited resources. *Now what do you do?*

Lao Tse seeks to lift us beyond the limits the body imposes, and restore our memory of our inherent spiritual nature. If you think you are a body only, you are ruled by its demands and restrictions, and your life is reduced to a daily struggle to get enough. You think you are here to simply eat, sleep, have sex, protect your territory, and fight for stuff. You identify with your smallness and overlook your magnitude. But if you know there is more to you than what's encapsulated by your skin, you have access to infinite resources and rewards that bodies alone cannot grasp.

> *The five colors blind the eye.*
> *The five tones deafen the ear.*
> *The five flavors dull the taste.*
> *Racing and hunting madden the mind,*
> *Precious things lead us astray.*
>
> —— *12*

Lao Tse identifies absorption in the physical plane as a distraction from our true purpose. *Tao Te Ching* would have us appreciate the physical world for the beauties and gifts it bestows, but not to the extent that we forget our greater reality.

"Racing and hunting" refers to chasing the stuff the world deems precious—possessions, money, fame, power, prestige, and the most Twitter followers. The sage, on the other hand, looks *within* for her treasure. She plumbs the depths of the soul rather than seeking external approval. She realizes that life is lived from within out, and the source of her life is Spirit. She trusts that by seeing beyond the things of the world, she will lose nothing and gain everything.

Embrace Your Humanity

Some spiritual teachings identify the body as evil and exhort us to deny, squelch, fight, and even mutilate the body. Some religions prescribe self-punishment and self-flagellation. Religious or not, many of us treat our bodies worse than our car or our pets. We keep working without resting, forget to eat or eat food with empty or harmful ingredients, put ourselves in toxic environments, engage in physical or emotional combat, and put up with lack and pain because we have been taught that self-denial is noble. "It must be God's will that I suffer," we tell ourselves. Lao Tse would have none of this. Instead, he would have us make peace with our body, treat it with kindness and respect, and bring it into harmony with the Tao, which wants only our happiness.

Jesus taught compassion for the human experience. "If a man's son asked him for a piece of bread, would he give him a stone?" The Nazarene master performed the miracle of loaves and fishes to feed the multitudes. He did not tell the assembled masses, "If you were really spiritual, you would not need to eat." He healed the blind, deaf, and paralyzed, affirming that the Father wished physical well-being for them. He didn't say, "You need to suffer to pay off your karma," or "Just keep struggling now and one day you will be rewarded in heaven." He knew that *this* was the day they deserved heaven, right where they stood. Yet we make up all kinds of bizarre stories and illogical rationalizations about how and why we deserve to suffer. Meanwhile your angels and friends look on, shaking their heads, patiently waiting for you to love yourself as much as they love you. Jesus Christ would not wish suffering on anyone, and neither would Lao Tse.

Right Use of the Body

The body exists to experience and magnify the presence of love. It is a communication device through which higher truth is received and extended. The body is a means to an end, given to fulfill a purpose beyond itself. When you live in the Tao, the body functions in a healthy, serviceable fashion. Pain and illness are not the Tao's intention or plan for you. You have a higher destiny.

When the body becomes a goal unto itself, we deny our joy and lose sight of our purpose. By analogy, if you become obsessed with constantly polishing your car, keep it in the garage so it doesn't get dirty or dented, and devote your income to adding more and more fancy accoutrements, you are missing the point of the car and it will not serve you as intended. You are supposed to be enjoying where your car takes you, not worshipping the vehicle as a god unto itself. *A Course in Miracles* tells us that one of the obstacles to peace is the belief that the body is valuable for what it offers. In this scenario, the body becomes the *object* of life rather than a *tool* to live it. You end up serving the body rather than it serving you. Your life becomes about glorifying and adorning the body rather than connecting with others. While the body is intended to *enhance* connection, when misused it *inhibits* connection. Real relationships are not about bodies. They are about spirit. You may have a dear friend who lives thousands of miles away, whom you see only rarely. Yet if you are joined in spirit, you are very much together. You are in their heart, and they in yours. Likewise, if a loved one departs this world and you believe that you and that person are bodies only, you will feel alone, abandoned, and bereft. But if you realize that person is a spiritual being who lives beyond the limits of the body, and so are you, you will recognize that your relationship continues and expands. Although my parents passed on many years ago, my sense of their presence and my communication with them has only deepened. They remain real and alive to me. Life is about love, and love does not depend on bodies.

Bodies, however, depend on love. Where there is love, bodies thrive and we fulfill our purpose of connection. Where love is absent, bodies wither and die. They may still walk the world, but their eyes grow hollow, their hearts cold, and life force diminishes to a mere trickle. Restore love, and the bodies thrive again. I saw a documentary about a little African boy who was wandering the streets naked and starving because his parents had abandoned him. Kindhearted people adopted the emaciated child on the brink of death, fed him, and nursed him back to life. While the initial photos were heartbreaking, ultimately he was restored to full health and vitality and went on to live a joyful, rewarding life. Love is the great healer that fills the emptiness of the world, restores vitality to the depleted, and makes a hell of an earth like unto heaven.

All things arise from Tao.
They are nourished by Virtue.
They are formed from matter.
They are shaped by environment.
Thus the ten thousand things respect Tao
and honor Virtue . . .

— 51

Priorities in Order

We can summarize the proper relationship between body and spirit with one simple word: *priorities.* Which comes first: Love or stuff? Connecting or dividing? Winning or joining? You don't have to slice away or deny your bodily activities. Just keep them in order. Go out to a sumptuous dinner with a friend. Just be sure your evening is more about being with your friend than your dinner. Wear attractive clothes, but remember that quality people are more impressed by your heart than your dress. Have rocking sex, but be sure you are making love to a person more than a form. Any intention that distances you from connection thwarts the Tao from delivering your gifts.

One day your body will disappear. But your soul will not. Body in service of soul, not the opposite. When that priority is in order, everything your body needs will show up by a hand greater than your own.

"What are you doing?" Lao Tse asked me.

"I'm building my body," I told him, as I clutched the specially weighted stones and pumped my arms to firm my biceps. "There's a fellow in my town who has an amazing physique. Muscles everywhere. All the girls flock around him. I want to have a body as strong and attractive as his."

"I see," said the master, the wheels in his mind turning.

A few weeks later Lao Tse invited me to join him at a stage play in a nearby city. When I heard that the star of the show was Na Liu, I nearly went through the roof. Na Liu was considered the most beautiful and talented actress in the province. She was terribly sexy, the fantasy of all the men who saw her dance.

When the big night came, I was thrilled that Lao Tse and I had been given front-row seats. Na Liu was indeed gorgeous; it was easy to understand why she was so popular. After the play an usher came to us. "Master Lao Tse, Miss Liu heard you were in the audience tonight, and she would like to meet you."

Lao Tse nodded humbly. He certainly wasn't enamored with the actress like I was, but he usually took an invitation as a sign that the Tao was guiding him, and accepted. As you can imagine, I was close behind.

The usher led us to Miss Liu's dressing room, where she stood and greeted the master. Then she began to bark orders to her assistants to make a place for us on the couch and get us drinks. We sat and Na Liu talked with Lao Tse for a while. But the interaction was not much of a conversation. In contrast to most people who wanted to learn from the master and asked him questions about their spiritual path, Miss Liu spent most of the time bragging about her performances and awards, and berating actresses she considered her competition. Lao Tse listened politely for a while, and then at the first opportunity excused us.

When we were outside the theater Lao Tse asked me, "What did you think of Na Liu?"

"She certainly is beautiful and I enjoyed her performance. But when we met her I have to say I was disappointed. I found her to be self-absorbed and mean-spirited."

Lao Tse nodded. "Her body is attractive but her soul is wounded. She is lovely to the eyes, but leaves the heart hungry," he simply said, and left it at that.

A month later the master invited me to join him to meet a longtime friend of his. We found our way to the house of Lihua Wei, a very old woman. Her body was frail and her skin quite wrinkled, but when she answered the door I sensed immense joy and delight emanating from her. Immediately I felt lifted and I was eager to be in her presence.

As we sat for tea with Lihua, after a few minutes I completely forgot that she bore many marks of age. I was in the presence of a vital, engaged, spirited young woman. I felt so happy with her that I did not want to leave.

Lao Tse finally announced that we had to go, and we departed.

"What did you think of Lihua?" he asked me.

"What a radiant spirit! I felt so enlivened being with her."

Lao Tse nodded. "Now you have met a woman with a beautiful body but an empty soul, and a woman with an aged body and a vivacious soul. What do you think about bodybuilding now?"

The master's question took me off guard. I wasn't expecting to make that connection at that moment. I gave it some thought.

"I guess real beauty is of the spirit, not the body."

Lao Tse smiled. "A lesson well learned."

"Does that mean I should quit bodybuilding?"

The master shrugged. "Not necessarily. If you enjoy it and it makes you feel good, fine. It's a healthy discipline. Just don't make your body a god. Would you rather end up with a woman like Na Liu, or one like Lihua Wei?"

My answer didn't take much thought. "I want to end up with a woman with a beautiful soul, no matter how her body looks."

The master proudly patted me on the upper arm. "Wow, quite a muscle you have here," he noticed. "Let's get you back to the cabin so you can stack some wood."

Leaf Medicine

Everything your body needs to maintain its health and well-being has been given as a gift from the earth. While human beings have manufactured a sprawling arsenal of pharmaceuticals, the natural world provides simpler and healthier means of healing. Indigenous people know the specific healing qualities of plants in the wild. To a knowledgeable native, a walk through the jungle is a visit to a huge natural pharmacopoeia. When I lived in Fiji, I was working in the forest near my house with a native Fijian. At one point I cut my hand and it started to bleed. When I told him I was going back to the house to get some antibiotics and a Band-Aid, he told me, "Wait one moment." He walked to a tree, tore off a leaf, and rubbed it on the cut, which stopped the bleeding immediately. "My father taught me about leaf medicine," he told me. "Your hand will be fine." And it was.

At other times I have taken antibiotics, for which I am also grateful. While it may be popular in the holistic health community to decry the evils of Western medicine, allopathy provides many healing modalities we should be thankful for and bless. God works through medical doctors. Surgeries and pharmaceuticals have saved and extended many lives. If a physician and drugs have relieved you of pain and diminished your symptoms, you must respect their effects as an act of grace. Not long ago, people would have died of ailments that medicine routinely treats today. Let us give honor where it is due. Allopathy is an instrument of the Tao.

At the same time, a significant portion of Western medicine is invasive and yields harmful side effects. Some statistics cite improperly administered drugs and surgery as the third leading cause of death in our nation. We cannot isolate and treat one part of the body without recognizing that organ's relationship to the whole person. The Tao is not hasty to get rid of troublesome organs. Instead, it would address mind, body, and spirit as a harmonious unit with interdependent parts. Would it not be preferable to be healed by simple, natural, inexpensive ingredients as remedies directly from our brilliant planet rather than piercing the body and ingesting ingredients that cause a different kind of harm? Use allopathic techniques where you need them, but go natural where you can.

When someone needs medical aid in China, a country with thousands of years of experience with natural healing, that person goes to a clinic where one door leads to modern medicine, and the other to ancient healing methods. The patient then chooses the type of treatment he or she prefers. In our nation we have made some small strides toward this choice; allopathic physicians are gaining more respect for natural remedies. A friend of mine is a nurse in a hospital where more and more doctors are recommending medical marijuana for treatment of disease. Yet we still have a long way to go before natural healing stands fully side by side with Western medicine. As more and more people experience the benefits of "leaf medicine," it will become more accepted and popular. The Tao reveals itself by the tangible results it obtains.

Medicine of the future will depend less on manipulation of symptoms and more on healing at our core. It will be based more on consciousness than instruments. We will heal with light, sound, the power of the mind, prayer, and gifts from the earth. We will focus less on isolated elements of our lives and more on lifestyle. Our natural state is ease. The word *disease* is aptly named. *Disease* means that we have dissed ease. The Tao is all about ease. When we move away from the Tao, disease directs us to rejoin it. All illness is a call for a course correction. When we figure out what that correction is and we step into it, we have reclaimed ease and the dis-ease can dissolve.

How Simple Can Healing Get?

Let's look at the primary methods we can use to keep our body in tune with the Tao, stay healthy, and feel good. While these techniques may seem obvious, many of us have become distracted or alienated from them and we need reminders of how simple the path of wellness can be.

1. Breathe.

While we are all breathing all the time, we rarely breathe deeply and we do not breathe pure air. When you become tense, your breathing becomes shallow. When you are relaxed and happy, your breathing goes deep. You can stimulate relaxation and joy by purposely breathing deeply.

The Earth in its original state was rich in oxygen far beyond the levels we experience today. Forests covered most of the planet and pumped life-enhancing oxygen into our atmosphere. As a result, all living things thrived far beyond today's norm. In Australia I saw a life-size statue of a prehistoric 12-foot kangaroo. In Florida I visited a museum displaying a replica of an ancient armadillo the size of a Volkswagen Beetle. In Chicago's O'Hare airport I stood under a full-size replica of a Brachiosaurus, whose head was over 30 feet high. My head at six feet high barely touched its knee! In days of yore, oxygen made everything healthy—and huge.

The world we have manufactured in opposition to the Tao has significantly depleted our atmosphere of oxygen. We've cut down forests, spewed hydrocarbons into the atmosphere, and we spend full days inside buildings with no fresh air. It's no wonder that so many people feel ill and irritable. Poor health and fleeting happiness are not the way the Tao intended for us to live.

Give your body the oxygen it needs by doing deep breathing exercises as taught in yoga, engaging in robust exercise, and placing yourself in oxygen-rich environments like the seashore, mountains, or any pristine natural setting. You will be amazed at how much better you feel, how your mind clears, and how your emotions balance when you simply breathe properly.

2. Eat well.

It's not just eating that keeps you alive. It's *what* you eat and *how* you eat. Eat foods as close to their natural state as possible, organic when you can. Avoid highly processed foods that don't look anything like they did when they sprang from the earth. Foods that are frozen, boiled, or shipped halfway around the planet lose much of their nutritional value. Our foods have also been so injected with chemicals and preservatives that what is supposed to give us life becomes toxic. Read labels and don't consume anything containing an ingredient you can't pronounce. Avoid refined sugars that create unnatural cravings and addictions. Don't consume meat with additives or that derive from animals grown in inhumane conditions. To purify your system and flush toxins, drink lots of clean, pure water.

When eating, honor your body by being relaxed and giving your meal proper attention. Eating on the run or while driving, working, standing, or doing business minimizes the sustenance your body receives. In our culture it has become the norm to eat fast food and eat food fast, and we have paid a price. Other cultures honor mealtimes. Italians, for example, take hours for lunch, gather with family and friends, cook elaborate meals, sip wine leisurely, and make mealtime one of the highlights of the day.

Receiving food is a metaphor for receiving love. People with eating disorders have difficulty receiving love, which manifests as an inability to receive food. The cure for eating disorders is to deepen one's capacity to receive love. Give yourself love by giving yourself good food and enjoying it.

3. Rest wisely.

The Tao is all about balance. If you are constantly going, going, going and doing, doing, doing without taking proper rest, you are out of balance. Give yourself enough time to sleep at night, and don't be shy to take naps during the day if you can. Quit working evenings and weekends. Some religions wisely prescribe a Sabbath—one day a week during which you put the busyness of life aside and renew your spirit.

A healthy lake needs an inlet and an outlet. If the lake has no inlet, it will dry up. If it has no outlet, it will flood. The balance of renewal and expression form the rhythm of life. Don't feel guilty about saying no to excessive work. Turn down invitations for social obligations that drain you.

When you return to work after resting well, you will be far more effective than if you had just kept working. Rest is one of the greatest contributions to personal and professional success.

> *Retire when the work is done;*
> *this is the way of heaven.*
> *— 9*

4. Move.

The body wants to enjoy the circulation of life force. Do something every day to get you out of your head and into your physical experience. Do yoga or tai chi, work out, walk, jog, engage in sport, hike, garden—anything that puts your body into action. You will feel better and think more clearly.

Bothersome issues will take on a refreshed perspective and you will see how to resolve them.

When I wrote my first book I decided to hole up for two weeks to finish it. I rented a cabin and wrote for many hours a day. It was not long before I was going buggy. I needed to balance my intense mental work with physical activity. So I went to the park and jogged miles each day. When I returned I was sane again and my writing went better. Activating your body will up-level your attitude and emotions. Even half an hour of movement can achieve this. While you are a spiritual being at your core, you must be a good steward for the steed that carries you through your earthly journey.

5. Minimize and manage stress.

Many of us have lots of plates spinning. We have jobs, kids, projects, and a ton of responsibilities, often to the point of overwhelm. We may even come to accept stress as required. It is not. A certain amount of busyness is healthy. Beyond that point it damages our health. Many of us are prone to take on more than we need to. Begin to slice away elements of your life that cause too much stress. "You can always do one thing less than you think you can." Set boundaries that protect your health and peace of mind.

Build stress-relieving activities into your schedule. Set aside time daily to journal, walk in nature, or get a massage. Engage in your inspired artistic hobby. Plan weekend trips, take vacations, and attend uplifting seminars and retreats. Make these soul-renewing activities as important as your work and other obligations. If you do not, the stressful activities will encroach and you will not find the precious time to do the things you love.

Notice when your body begins to give you a signal that you have stepped over a line into overwhelm. You probably have a part of your body that signals impending burnout. You may get a headache, a tickle in your throat, or indigestion. Such symptoms are messages from the Tao telling you that you have just gone past an important boundary. You are being guided to stop and renew. Honor these red flags calling you to restore yourself.

If you don't heed them, they can lead to accidents and diseases. Be open to messages from the universe showing you what you need to do to get and stay well. The Tao is on your team and it needs your cooperation.

6. Follow joy.

When you do what makes you happy, your body naturally infuses itself with hormones and nutrients that boost your immune system and foster robust health. In the film comedy *Ferris Bueller's Day Off,* Ferris phones his buddy Cameron to invite him to go out for a day of adventure. A sick Cameron groans, "I'm dying." Ferris replies, "You're not dying. You just can't think of anything good to do." This line embodies a profound truth: When you are living your joyful purpose, you manifest energy and vitality. If you feel sick and tired, ask yourself, *What am I sick and tired of?* Then, *What joy have I been denying myself?* Your answers to these questions inscribe your personal map to healing. The Tao wants you to feel good and be effective. When you act on that intention, that is exactly what will happen.

Conscious Departure

When we are done using our body, we can release it to return to the elements it came from and allow our spirit to once again become its essential self. How we go through that process is as crucial as how we live. While many people depart fearfully or unconsciously, some people depart consciously. We have been trained by word and example to believe that death must be difficult. But there are people who exit gracefully. Scott Nearing was a pioneer in the healthy living movement. He and his wife Helen left their city life in the 1930s, built their home in natural Vermont, grew organic food, and established one of the first modern models of sustainable living. Their book *Living the Good Life* has become an eco-classic. Scott lived until the age of 100, and, I am told, he exited quite gracefully. He gradually stopped eating, then he went to juices, then to water, and then to nothing. Then he gently slipped out of his vehicle and disappeared into the heart of God.

We have been taught that when we are ready to exit stage left, we need a disease as an excuse to depart. But it is not so. We can leave in a gentle, peaceful manner if we so choose. Abraham-Hicks offers the model, "Happy, healthy, happy, healthy, happy, healthy—dead."

The body is the garment we wear to journey through life, called by some "an earth suit." Just as you would not want to wear the same shirt forever, you would not want to wear the same body. Danish theologian Søren Kierkegaard said, "Indeed if there was a man who could not die, would he not be the unhappiest of men?" At some point we tire of playing in the world of separate forms and we are ready to go home. If we can learn to live with ease and grace, we can depart with ease and grace. Then the arms of love will embrace us and we will regain the vitality of spirit unencumbered by "the surly bonds of earth."

Misfortune comes from having a body.

Without a body, how could there be misfortune?

Surrender yourself humbly; then you can be trusted to care for all things.

Love the world as your own self; then you can truly care for all things.

—— 13

The body lives because the breath of the Tao is infused into it. When that spirit is withdrawn, the body will die. Yet the spirit will live on more surely than the sun will rise tomorrow. The Tao is less concerned with what happens after death than what happens during life. If we live well, we will die well, and we will merge gloriously back into All That Is. While we walk the earth, quality of life is more crucial than quantity of life. When we stray from the Tao, what is supposed to be life becomes death. When we reclaim the Tao, the reality of life eclipses the illusion of death. The purpose of life is not to arrive safely at death. It is to live. *Tao Te Ching* offers us the soundest advice of how to make our time in a body truly worthwhile, rise beyond limits, and dwell in a peace that passes understanding.

> *Being divine, you will be at one with the Tao.*
> *Being at one with the Tao is eternal.*
> *And though the body dies, the Tao*
> *will never pass away.*
>
> — 16

EPILOGUE

There were just a few of us by his side when he breathed his last. He lived his life without ostentation and he did not wish his departure to be any more dramatic.

As I sat by his side and held his hand, he asked me for a sip of water. Lao Tse lifted his head while I held the cup to his lips. Part of me felt deeply saddened to see my master go. I selfishly feared having to forge through the rest of my life without his benevolent guidance. How much time and suffering had he saved me?

Another part of me realized that the Tao was operating impeccably even in the face of the appearance of loss. The master had promised me that after he departed he would whisper in my ear when I needed him. I took comfort in the hope that he had spoken truly.

Finishing the drink, Lao Tse offered a small smile. I assumed he was too weak to talk, but he surprised me with a few words: "Trust the Tao, my friend. It will not fail you."

With that, he let his head fall back on the pillow and closed his eyes. He took a long breath in, and breathed out. He did not breathe in again. I watched carefully as his chest stilled. After a minute I knew he was gone.

A tear came to my eye. I had hoped to be stronger, but with Lao Tse's guidance I had learned to accept my grief as well as my joy. My dear friend was with me no more.

Another friend in attendance pulled the sheet up over Lao Tse's face. This day would be the last time I looked into his eyes or saw his gracious smile.

I sat with the master for a few more minutes, wishing him well on his journey into the light. I took comfort in thinking that he had returned unto the Tao he so loved. This cranky old body that had ceased to serve him would encumber him no more. At one time he told me he had seen people who had passed on, and in spirit they appeared about 19 years of age, at the peak of their vitality. I imagined Lao Tse at 19. If that is who he had become, I was happy for him.

I said a final good-bye, stood, and left the room. I forced myself to keep breathing deeply to try to absorb what had just happened. Then I heard him call my name. I turned to see if he had somehow come back to life. But there was no movement. He was gone.

I stepped outside, sat on a large rock, and looked back at his little house. He had told me he wanted me to live there after he was gone. At first I felt unworthy to accept, but then I realized that the master was giving me his final gift to demonstrate he saw more in me than I saw in myself. I have endeavored to live up to his faith in me and maintain the tranquil energy Lao Tse imbued in that simple abode.

Now every morning as chilly mountain winds assail the eastern wall of the cabin, I take refuge in the quiet space where the gusts of change cannot disturb the flame burning within. I make a cup of tea for the master and myself, I sit at the kitchen table across from his chair, and I converse with him. I talk to Lao Tse in my mind and he answers. He has not gone very far at all. Now he lives in my heart. In an odd way, he is even closer to me now. I think he would have wanted it that way.

ACKNOWLEDGMENTS

I humbly honor the spirit of the master Lao Tse, whether he was one person, or many, or a brilliant idea in the mind of the Tao. That vibrant soul has set forth a stream of truth that has flowed through the centuries and brought wisdom, solace, and guidance to a world hungry for healing, now more than ever.

My first copy of *Tao Te Ching* was the elegant edition by Gia-Fu Feng and Jane English, containing a stirring translation augmented by simple black-and-white nature photographs. That book has stayed close to me for many years, and I deeply wish to honor the translators.

My beloved Dee remains my steadfast supporter and encourager. For her dedication to this work I am humbly and eternally grateful.

To my dogs who keep me sane, thank you for jumping onto my lap when I am writing and reminding me what's real.

What a treat to work with my dear editor at Hay House, Anne Barthel, a gently wise co-visionary who calls forth the best through me.

To all the good people at Hay House, including visionary founder Louise Hay, CEO Reid Tracy, publisher Patty Gift, art team members Tricia Breidenthal and Caroline DiNofia, interior designer Nick Welch, and all the other talented creative and promotional teams—what a blessing to work with such kind, caring, efficient, creative people. As always, it is a treat to work with everyone at Hay House Radio.

And to you, dear reader, I thank and honor you for receiving the wisdom seeded within you, and making Lao Tse's transmission complete.

ABOUT THE
AUTHOR

Alan Cohen, M.A., holds degrees in Psychology and Human Organizational Development. He is the author of 27 popular inspirational books, including the best-selling *A Course in Miracles Made Easy* and the award-winning *A Deep Breath of Life*. He is a contributing writer for the #1 *New York Times* best-selling series Chicken Soup for the Soul, and he is featured in the book *101 Top Experts Who Help Us Improve Our Lives*. His books have been translated into 30 foreign languages.

Alan's radio show *Get Real* airs weekly on Hay House Radio, and his monthly column From the Heart is published in magazines internationally. His work has been presented on CNN and Oprah.com and in *USA Today*, *The Washington Post*, and *Huffington Post*. He is a primary presenter in the award-winning documentary *Finding Joe*, as well as other inspirational videos.

Alan is the founder and director of the Foundation for Holistic Life Coaching. He also keynotes and presents seminars on themes of life mastery, spiritual development, and vision psychology. He resides with his family in Hawaii.

For information on Alan Cohen's books, seminars, life coach training, DVDs, CDs, videos, and online courses, visit www.AlanCohen.com.

LEARN MORE
WITH ALAN COHEN

If you have enjoyed and benefited from *The Tao Made Easy*, you may want to deepen your understanding and inspiration by participating in Alan Cohen's in-person seminars, online courses, life coach training, or online subscription programs.

Quote for the Day—An inspirational quotation e-mailed to you each day (free)

Monthly e-Newsletter—Uplifting articles and announcements of events (free)

Wisdom for Today—A stimulating life lesson e-mailed to you daily

Live Webinars—Interactive uplifting programs on topics relevant to the Tao, self-empowerment, and holistic living

Online Courses—In-depth experiential exploration of *A Course in Miracles*, relationships, prosperity, healing, prayer, metaphysics, and time management

Life Coach Training—Become a certified professional life coach or enhance your career and personal life with coaching skills

Mastery Training—A transformational retreat in Hawaii to align your life with your passion, power, and purpose

For information about all of these programs and new products and events, visit www.AlanCohen.com.

Hay House Titles of Related Interest

YOU CAN HEAL YOUR LIFE, the movie, starring Louise Hay & Friends
(available as a 1-DVD program, an expanded 2-DVD set, and an
online streaming video)
Learn more at www.hayhouse.com/louise-movie

THE SHIFT, the movie,
starring Dr. Wayne W. Dyer
(available as a 1-DVD program, an expanded 2-DVD set, and an
online streaming video)
Learn more at www.hayhouse.com/the-shift-movie

***

*LIFE ON EARTH: Understanding Who We Are, How We Got Here,
and What May Lie Ahead,* by Mike Dooley

MORE BEAUTIFUL THAN BEFORE: How Suffering Transforms Us,
by Steve Leder

SACRED POWERS: The Five Secrets to Awakening Transformation,
by davidji

*SECRETS OF THE LOST MODE OF PRAYER: The Hidden Power of
Beauty, Blessing, Wisdom, and Hurt,* by Gregg Braden

*SPONTANEOUS CREATIVITY: Meditations for Manifesting Your
Positive Qualities,* by Tenzin Wangyal Rinpoche

All of the above are available at your local bookstore,
or may be ordered by contacting Hay House (see next page).

***

We hope you enjoyed this Hay House book. If you'd like to receive our online catalog featuring additional information on Hay House books and products, or if you'd like to find out more about the Hay Foundation, please contact:

Hay House, Inc., P.O. Box 5100, Carlsbad, CA 92018-5100
(760) 431-7695 or (800) 654-5126
(760) 431-6948 (fax) or (800) 650-5115 (fax)
www.hayhouse.com® • www.hayfoundation.org

———

Published in Australia by: Hay House Australia Pty. Ltd.,
18/36 Ralph St., Alexandria NSW 2015
Phone: 612-9669-4299 • *Fax:* 612-9669-4144
www.hayhouse.com.au

Published in the United Kingdom by: Hay House UK, Ltd.,
The Sixth Floor, Watson House, 54 Baker Street, London W1U 7BU
Phone: +44 (0)20 3927 7290 • *Fax:* +44 (0)20 3927 7291
www.hayhouse.co.uk

Published in India by: Hay House Publishers India,
Muskaan Complex, Plot No. 3, B-2, Vasant Kunj, New Delhi 110 070
Phone: 91-11-4176-1620 • *Fax:* 91-11-4176-1630
www.hayhouse.co.in

———

Access New Knowledge.
Anytime. Anywhere.

Learn and evolve at your own pace
with the world's leading experts.

www.hayhouseU.com

Listen. Learn. Transform.

Reach your fullest potential with unlimited Hay House audios!

Gain access to endless wisdom, inspiration, and encouragement from world-renowned authors and teachers—guiding and uplifting you as you go about your day. With the *Hay House Unlimited* Audio app, you can learn and grow in a way that fits your lifestyle . . . and your daily schedule.

With your membership, you can:

- Let go of old patterns, step into your purpose, live a more balanced life, and feel excited again.

- Explore thousands of audiobooks, meditations, immersive learning programs, podcasts, and more.

- Access exclusive audios you won't find anywhere else.

- Experience completely unlimited listening. No credits. No limits. No kidding.

Try for FREE!

Visit **hayhouse.com/listen-free** to start your free trial and get one step closer to living your best life.

Printed in the United States
by Baker & Taylor Publisher Services